JACK DOMINIAN

JACK DOMINIAN

Lay Prophet?

JOCK DALRYMPLE

GEOFFREY
CHAPMAN

Geoffrey Chapman
A Cassell imprint
Villiers House, 41/47 Strand, London WC2N 5JE
387 Park Avenue South, New York, NY 10016-8810

First published 1995
.
British Library Cataloguing-in-Publication Data
A catalogue record for this book is available from the British Library.

ISBN 0-225-66733-9

Cover photographs © Jack Dominian
Author photograph © Jock Dalrymple

Typeset by Colset Pte Ltd, Singapore
Printed and bound in Great Britain by
Biddles Ltd, Guildford and King's Lynn

Contents

FOR MY PARENTS
as they celebrate their ruby wedding,
and all who have sustained, healed
and encouraged me to grow

Foreword

I remember my mother, I think in the early 1950s, refusing to speak to an acquaintance she met in the street who had just been divorced. Yet my mother was a liberal with a particular concern for the underdog. What she still considered heinous then has today become so accepted that in Britain a third of new marriages are dissolved. Meanwhile, an increasing number of couples choose to cohabit without benefit of clergy. The institution of marriage is under threat.

During the 1960s, when the end of deference was felt as a new freedom, allowing young people in particular to 'do their own thing', these trends were not questioned in the way they are now. Both in the United States and in Britain, there has been an awakening at the perceived danger to the cohesion of society. A battery of research studies has shown how children tend to suffer psychologically, socially and economically if they do not have a stable family background. Particularly significant has been the reconversion of significant circles of the Left to the importance of the family unit and the rediscovery by them that most children will benefit from being brought up in a stable environment with two parents. At the same time, the opinion persists, more or less vociferously expressed, that there can be no going back to the model of marriage as a contract, based on fixed roles for father and mother as breadwinner and housewife respectively.

Sigmund Freud warned that what is not understood is destined to be repeated, and one of those who has worked hardest to try to understand what is happening to marriage so as to save it as an institution is Dr Jack Dominian, the subject of this book. He is both a practising psychiatrist who observes marriage as a secular phenomenon, and a practising Catholic who believes that marriage is a divine mystery. The joint use of these two very different tools of understanding is part of the interest of any study of his thought.

Long before the care and maintenance of marriage became an everyday topic, Jack Dominian was analysing the relationship between the spouses on which everything else depends. As Jock Dalrymple points out, this fundamental aspect has taken up his attention to such an extent as to risk excluding elements of the wider picture, but by going to the heart of the matter he has been able to throw a concentrated ray of light which has been an illumination for many. He has also been able to make recommendations to the State and the Churches about how to support marriage which have at last found a hearing.

He has been criticized for presenting marriage, and the sexual side of it in particular, in terms which are too idealistic. No doubt he tends to. He refuses to stand in judgement over the massive shift in the understanding of marriage, but rather accepts it and welcomes it. It is this which marks him off most clearly from some moral reformers whose own prescriptions for the future envisage a wholesale condemnation of present trends. He is optimistic, in line with his Christian faith.

The influence of Christianity on the understanding of marriage in the West has been enormous, and the influence of St Augustine greatest of all. Whereas in the East a succession of great doctors of the Church correct and complement each other, in the West Augustine towers above everybody else. Inevitably the impact of one man's thought must be one-sided, and the doctrine of marriage has both benefited and suffered. It is Dr Dominian's belief that most people look for God today in their relationships, and that the Christian Church has to learn afresh how to speak to their condition.

In his view the Catholic Church has been well equipped to do so by the reforms of the Second Vatican Council. He sees the recovery of Catholic humanism at Vatican II as having revolutionary implications for the doctrine of marriage, and I was surprised to discover from this book just how far across the spectrum he has moved since the days when he condemned contraception as evil. In particular he has been influenced by the Second Vatican Council's document on the Church in the modern world, *Gaudium et Spes*, whose opening words could stand for his own approach: 'The joys and the hopes, the griefs and the anxieties of the men and women of this age, especially those who are poor or in any way afflicted, these too are the joys and hopes, the griefs and anxieties of the followers of Christ. Indeed, nothing genuinely human fails to raise an echo in their hearts.'

He regrets that the Catholic Church has not so far developed the Council's more positive and holistic treatment of marriage as fully as it should, indeed that it has gone back on some of the insights that were then achieved. As a result, he sees an alarming chasm opening up between the attitudes of Church and world. It is a relief to find the truth bluntly stated. In defence of his prophetic outspokenness, he appeals to the Council's encouragement to individual lay people to express their opinions 'on things which concern the good of the Church' if they have 'knowledge, confidence or ability' which is particularly relevant. It is in the field of sex and marriage that the exclusion from the Catholic teaching authority of the full input of laymen and women has most clearly held back the Church's doctrine.

A time of fierce social change like the present is disorientating and alarming for everyone. It is easy to lose confidence and heart. Jack Dominian has been a pathfinder, enabling many others to take their bearings. Jock Dalrymple's sympathetic but searching appraisal will be of interest both to those who are familiar with Dr Dominian's work, and to others who have not previously come across it.

John Wilkins
Editor, *The Tablet*

Introduction

In *The Tablet* of 12 December 1992 an American priest, Thomas Faucher, wrote a short article entitled 'Outsiders need not apply'. He began by introducing three characters: Monica, a 28-year-old, with three children by two different ex-husbands, who worked nights and most weekends; Theo, a 40-year-old, who went from job to job, had no permanent home and had been married a couple of times; and 'Bookend', a street kid, who lived part of the time with his girlfriend and part of the time with his grandmother. All three wanted to become Catholics; the point of the article was to illustrate how difficult it would be for any of them actually to do so because, in the opinion of the author, present-day Catholic rules and regulations were made for 'stable middle-class people with free Wednesday evenings and free Sunday mornings'.

Two paragraphs in the article particularly struck me.

> Monica, Theo and Bookend are poor people. They are poor not only financially, but socially, educationally, and in lack of stability. They are the modern poor, with many marriages, children by different partners, fuzzy relationships, and no schedules.

> There is supposed to be a special place at the eucharistic table for the poor, not just the economically poor, but especially the socially and morally poor. Jesus did not say to the woman caught in adultery, 'Go and take two years of classes, and then apply for your annulments. When that is done, come back and we will talk about the possible next steps.' There is something wrong. How can it be that rules, regulations, processes are making it so difficult for the poor to become the Church?

That article might seem to have little connection with a book on Jack Dominian and his vision of sexuality and marriage. It was, however, one of the final pieces in a very personal jigsaw, and, as I shall try to explain, one that helped to convince me of the potential value of writing this book.

The first pieces in this jigsaw began to slot into place sometime between 19 July 1986, when I was ordained a priest in my home town of North Berwick on the east coast of Scotland, and 22 August, when I was asked to go 20 miles up the road towards Edinburgh, to be the assistant priest in a parish on the outskirts of the city. When I arrived there, I was probably even more naïve than most newly ordained clergy; certainly I had had very limited pastoral experience. However, both the parish priests and the parishioners were patient and kind, and then tolerant, and the four years I spent there were extremely happy and formative ones.

With my lack of experience, one of the things I had worried about was how to respond if parishioners came to me with sexual difficulties or dilemmas. My anxiety was wasted energy. Sex was not an issue; or rather, as it became clear in my first year in the parish, the vast majority of parishioners no longer looked to the priest, if they ever had, for guidance on such matters. Church teaching in this area was perceived by them as being so out of touch with reality that it had lost credibility.

Halfway through my first year there, the parish began a series of Parish Renewal Weekends, as part of a diocesan programme. These were very intense, often exhilarating, always exhausting experiences — 20 or 30 parishioners and two priests locked up in the church hall for a full 48 hours, or so it seemed, praying, sharing, eating and drinking together; they proved so popular that we organized seven of them in the next twelve months.

These weekends had an enormous influence on me because they offered me a first prolonged opportunity as a priest really to listen to people's joys and sorrows, to what their faith meant to them and to their experience of the Church, both positive and negative. I was deeply moved by much of what I heard. In particular, my eyes were opened to something I had previously hardly been aware of — the pain and rejection felt by so many Catholics who, because of their marital status, were unable to receive the sacraments. At least one member of the group on each of our last four or five weekends was either in a second marriage themselves, or was married to someone who had been married before. Both Saturday and Sunday

evenings ended with Mass; for some reason, as the weekends progressed, these closing Masses became more and more highly-
charged, the non-communicant sitting silently, sometimes in tears,
the communicants increasingly upset and scandalized at what they
perceived to be the Church at its most harsh and unforgiving. So
many knew from their own experience, or the experience of close
family or friends, the sense of failure and anguish that so often
accompanies a broken marriage. There seemed to be unanimous
agreement that another rejection, this time at the hands of the
Church, was not justified — or indeed Christian.

I visited one or two of the non-communicants in the aftermath
of these weekends and, as a result, had my first experience of
conducting annulment interviews and setting annulment cases in
motion. These, too, made a lasting impression; I simply had not
anticipated how easily these interviews could reopen the wounds of
the past — even if in time I became aware how, in some situations,
they could also offer an opportunity for healing.

In addition I learnt, when I sent reports of the interviews to
the Scottish National Tribunal, that the limited resources allocated
to the Tribunal were such that it would be over three years before
these cases were officially opened and examined. That seemed
to me an additional injustice, especially as Canon Law specifically states that such cases should be dealt with within eighteen
months.

The parish was a warm lively responsive one. One of the things
that grew out of the Parish Renewal Weekends was the RCIA —
the Rite of Christian Initiation of Adults — the process by which
adults are now received into the Catholic Church. Each year a
number of people in the town wanted to become Catholics, but each
year there was a similar problem to that encountered at the renewal
weekends — and by Theo, Monica and Bookend: at least one
candidate was in a second marriage or was married to a person
who had been married before. Making tentative enquiries, we
discovered that although it did not seem to make sense liturgically,
they could legally be confirmed and received into the Catholic
Church at the Easter Vigil, as long as they didn't actually receive
communion!

This was patently far from ideal, but better than nothing, so we
went ahead under those conditions for two years. During Lent of
1990, however, we learnt that a request for clarification had gone
to Rome and that in consequence the 'loophole' that allowed this

'solution' had been closed. That meant that it was no longer officially possible to receive somebody who was in an invalid marriage, unless they or their partner obtained an annulment, they were willing to live as 'brother and sister' with each other, or they split up altogether.

A wise old priest once told me that it takes the average parishioner five years to get to know and trust their minister or priest; that might be an exaggeration but in my experience the principle holds true. Certainly, during my final two years in the parish more and more parishioners began to come and see me because they wanted to talk confidentially to someone — either about the difficulties they were experiencing in their marriage, or in the aftermath of a separation. A significant and lasting shift occurred in my outlook, and I began to see beyond Church rules, Church problems and apparently Church-induced pain, to an infinitely more widespread problem, the vast sea of human anguish that resulted from marital breakdown and divorce.

Confronted by so many painful situations, I could do little to help beyond provide a listening ear, useful as that was. After one particularly difficult encounter I made contact with CMAC — the Catholic Marriage Advisory Council — and with the couple's agreement arranged an appointment. It proved to be a turning-point for them, and for me. There was a good group of CMAC counsellors in Edinburgh, and I found myself increasingly acting as a bridge to them for several parishioners in dire need of support. In doing so I became aware of three factors: how difficult many people found it to pluck up courage to make and attend a first appointment; how men in general, and husbands and parish priests in particular, viewed both counselling and CMAC with great suspicion; and yet how enormously effective counselling could be in helping some couples to rebuild their marriage and in enabling others to begin to come to terms with the break-up of a relationship.

In addition CMAC also helped to train a team of 'marriage helpers' from the parish. My diocese had for some time insisted that if a couple were to be married in a Catholic church, they needed to give six months' notice and undergo a preparation course of six sessions with the priest. Whereas in the past this course had been 'instruction', focusing on the sacrament of marriage and on the Catholic faith in general, now it was tending to concentrate on the couple's relationship — a healthy shift from 'how to survive being married to a Catholic' to 'how to survive being married to each

other'. I had used a preparation programme from the Redemp-
torists involving questionnaires and tapes, and enjoyed getting to
know a couple reasonably well before their wedding day — but
increasingly I came to feel that this was an area which cried out for
lay involvement and leadership. With the help of CMAC and of a
skilled and sympathetic Natural Family Planning and fertility-
awareness expert we developed a friendly young team that ran three
fairly successful courses for engaged couples. However, although it
was good to be something other than a marital accident and
emergency service, it further heightened my awareness of the potential goodwill and experience in every community that was available
for the support of marriage but was simply not being mobilized.

Halfway through 1990 I was asked by my archbishop to go for
further study. He had a positive attitude to ongoing formation for
the clergy, and the diocesan seminary needed to train a new lecturer
in moral theology. As a consequence, I found myself at the beginning of October 1990 a somewhat unenthusiastic licentiate student
at the University of Leuven, 20 miles east of Brussels.

Before setting off for Leuven, I had met with my spiritual guide,
Roland Walls, to discuss topics for the thesis that was a part of the
licence degree. He had suggested that any subject that included an
analysis of the gap between the theory of Catholic teaching on
sexuality and marriage, and the reality of everyday life, would not
only be worthwhile and necessary, but would also provide some continuity with what had most struck me in my four years in the parish.
The next step was to search for a promoter from among the moral
theology professors, so I approached an impressively lively Flemish
Salesian, Roger Burggraeve, and explained to him the general area
I wanted to specialize in. He thought for a moment, went over to
his bookshelf, produced five Jack Dominian books and said 'I've
been looking for somebody to do some work on him; would you be
interested?'

I was immediately excited by the prospect. One of Dominian's
books, *Marriage, Faith and Love*, had lived for a long time in a
prominent spot next to my father's armchair at home, a sign of his
enthusiasm for Dominian for nearly two decades. I myself had gone
to listen to a talk Dominian gave in Oxford in 1976; and over the
years I had read many of his articles in *The Tablet*, several of which
seemed to address directly the questions provoked by my first years
as a pastoral priest.

A week later, the telephone rang. It was Roger Burggraeve: 'Are you free on Friday? Jack Dominian is in Brussels and is coming to Leuven for the afternoon; would you like to meet him?' Over coffee, Dominian expressed interest in the proposed thesis, promised to help in any way he could, and invited me to visit him at his Marriage Research Centre whenever I wanted.

Subsequent encounters with him and with his wife Edith — a much more forthcoming biographical source — gave me added enthusiasm for the project. Remarkably little had been written about Dominian the man, and yet he had had a most varied and fascinating early life. In addition, I learnt that although Dominian seemed to have been proclaiming much the same message for as long as I could remember, he had in fact been a very traditional Catholic until the early 1960s; and that it was as a result of his experiences listening to and counselling couples whose marriages were breaking up that he had undergone a kind of conversion and begun to challenge aspects of the Church's official stance in the area of sexuality and marriage.

The more I learnt about Jack Dominian, the more I began to look on him as a prophetic figure. As well as this 'conversion experience' and his deep sense of mission, both of which seemed to me prerequisites for a prophet, he had other important qualifications: his voice, as far as its impact on the Magisterium of the Catholic Church had been concerned, had been a voice crying in the wilderness. Similarly his attempts to encourage the government to respond more directly to the enormous increase in the divorce rate had been largely unsuccessful. At the same time, he was addressing supremely important issues, and working with all his might to find answers for questions that so many seemed to ignore. Why were so many marriages breaking down? What were the consequences? Did counselling make a difference? In what other ways could marriage be supported? How could the Church's teaching on sex, marriage and marital breakdown respond to these issues? How could it be communicated in such a way as to regain credibility in the eyes of the faithful and not-so-faithful? My thesis, completed in May 1992, was suitably hagiographic.

However, before I finally left Leuven, I spent some time at Trosly-Breuil, near Paris, where Jean Vanier had in 1964 founded his first l'Arche community for the mentally handicapped, and where he still lives. Vanier's personality and vision made an enormous impact. Studying Dominian, the great advocate of marriage, had left me as a celibate feeling both envious and an 'outsider'; he seemed from my subjective perspective to be implying that true fulfilment and self-realization could only really be found in a sexually harmonious marriage.

Vanier, at first sight, had a fair amount in common with Dominian. Both were intelligent laymen who, turning to the scriptures for inspiration and making use of the insights of the human sciences and of their own personal experience, had sought in their books to help people live good and fulfilled Christian lives.

However, despite these similarities, I soon discovered that Vanier offered a very different vision for life from Dominian. While Dominian focuses above all on married couples and on husbands and wives as individuals, Vanier's main concern is with those with learning difficulties, who are frequently unable to live normal married lives, and with those who have been called to live in community. While Dominian seeks to encourage individuals and couples towards wholeness and 'intactness', Vanier reveals the value of accepting one's woundedness and brokenness. While Dominian believes that human love is the main way to experience divine love, Vanier writes most movingly of the importance of a direct and personal relationship with Jesus; and while Dominian thinks that morality is identical for Christian and humanist alike, Vanier implies that faith makes an essential difference to one's understanding of it. Although I felt that in most respects their approaches were complementary rather than contradictory, my experiences at Trosly made me more guarded in my enthusiasm for the Dominian vision and more critical of aspects of his theology.

In September 1992 I returned to Scotland. By then, to my relief, a new lecturer in moral theology had been appointed to the diocesan seminary. Instead, I was asked to become a parish priest in Fife, in a parish combining the proud old town of Leslie with half the new town of Glenrothes. I was also appointed a diocesan liaison officer with CMAC and encouraged to train as a marriage counsellor myself.

In my first month back in the country, I was asked by a young couple if I would be willing to 'accompany' them in their relationship as a kind of spiritual guide. However, despite my hope that this request for positive support for a marriage might be a 'sign of the times', it was not long before I was facing more familiar challenges, very similar to those I had encountered in my first parish. Glenrothes, like all new towns, has an above-average rate of marital breakdown, and soon I was in regular contact with

CMAC, arranging counselling appointments for parishioners. Telephoning the National Tribunal in search of forms for a potential annulment, I was dismayed to discover that there was still a two-and-a-half-year waiting list for annulment cases. In addition, the first person who enquired about how to become a Catholic was in a second relationship, and theoretically not 'eligible'.

It was soon after this enquiry that I came across Thomas Faucher's article about Monica, Theo and Bookend. I mentioned at the beginning of this introduction that it was one of the final pieces in my own personal jigsaw. That was because it put into words what I had increasingly been feeling — that the Church was hamstrung in its efforts to respond to the modern poor, not least their need to belong to the Church, by its official teaching on sexuality and marriage.

It is very easy to be critical: hard cases make bad laws and there are no easy solutions to the dilemmas facing the Church in this area. Nevertheless, I still felt that in an age of increasing secularization when so many people were turning away from it, there seemed to be unnecessary barriers placed in the way of those who were drawn to the Church in their time of greatest need. I also believed that as a Church we were not listening enough to what people's real problems were, and were not responding effectively to the real human issues such as the social upheaval caused by marital breakdown; and that this was partly because we were too caught up in the agendas set by our own structures and rules.

It was these feelings that made me turn again to Jack Dominian. I had grown to admire the dogged determination that Dominian had shown for over thirty years in keeping the whole subject of marriage and sexuality 'on the boil' and in not allowing official pronouncements to escape unchallenged; and I had been struck by the way that despite his limitations Dominian offered a coherent alternative vision of this area of life to the vision of the official Church and by how he sincerely claimed to be doing so as a loyal Catholic. However, I had also become increasingly aware that his views had not in recent years received the same degree of respect or attention that they had been given in the 1970s and 1980s.

There were several reasons for this. One was partly the consequence of the symbolic status Dominian had had since the late 1960s as the longstanding champion of the anti-*Humanae Vitae* camp and the bogeyman of conservatives, new and old; this status had served to confirm many people's impression that he had been saying the same thing in the same way for so long that it was therefore no longer worth listening to him. In addition, Dominian has not always endeared himself by his tendency to present his case in a slightly simplistic 'the tradition is wrong and here is the right answer' mode; such an approach has not been helped by the manner in which some of his more recent books have shown signs of being written hastily, with many more assertions and generalizations than footnotes or references.

Moreover, there was a third, and in my opinion particularly significant, reason. Part of the strength of Dominian's overall vision lies in its comprehensive nature and the way it forms an organic whole. The accompanying weakness is his failure to distinguish between those elements which are the fruit of his unquestioned professional expertise, such as the sociological and psychological synthesis that creates a model of the marital lifecycle; and those elements which, although offered in the same magisterial tone, can be viewed as the speculations of an amateur theologian, as in his interpretation of what prayer involves for a married couple.

I felt that there was a real danger that because of these factors much of real value in Dominian's vision would be ignored by the Church. Yet, as Thomas Faucher had pointed out, there was something very wrong when there was no place in the Church for the 'modern poor' with 'their many marriages' and 'children by different partners'.

Dominian, more than anyone else, had helped me to understand the sociological and psychological background that explained such a situation and that challenged the Catholic understanding of both sexuality and marriage.

In consequence, I decided to write a book about him that would attempt to do three things. First, to place his writings in the context of his own 'journey of faith'; and that 'journey of faith' in the context of the journey made by the Church and by society in his lifetime. Secondly, to offer a lucid and concise presentation of his overall understanding of sexuality and marriage. Thirdly, it would attempt a critique of that vision, distinguishing between his insights and his blind spots, in order to assess his achievements. High among those achievements, in my personal opinion, is the combination of zeal and intuition that has driven him to try to understand and find responses to so many of the dilemmas which have dominated my own life as a pastoral priest — dilemmas which, ultimately, have instigated this book.

Acknowledgements

This book would not exist without Br Roland Walls of the Ecumenical Community of the Transfiguration in Roslin, Midlothian. In 1990, he encouraged me, in the postgraduate studies on which I was about to embark, to risk a journey into that minefield of life, theology and pastoral practice, sex and marriage; as the book has unfolded in the four years since then, he has remained my principal source of wisdom and inspiration.

Nor would it have come into being without the influence of Professor Dr Roger Burggraeve SDB of the Faculty of Moral Theology of the Catholic University of Leuven. He made the initial suggestion that I write about Jack Dominian and was a most stimulating promoter of the subsequent licence thesis.

Jack and Edith Dominian have been more than helpful at every stage in a lengthy process; patient during interviews, warmly hospitable in offering a bed for the night, and endlessly co-operative with a variety of requests.

Many other people have also been enormously kind and generous with their time and houses, and in making criticisms and suggestions at various stages. I would specially like to thank my parents, Cardinal Basil Hume, Duncan Dormor, Fr Edmund Dougan OFM, Olivia Dalrymple, Maggie Parham, Ian and Alison Thompson, Barbara Parham, Fr Tim McConville, Linh Hoang, Fr George Ratzmann, Adrian Aylward, Jeanette Knight, Sr Margaret Mary O'Meara, Ian and Jane Petrie, Charlotte Wemyss, Patrick Ford, Fr Charlie Barclay, Fr Norman Cooper, Fr Gerry Hand, Fr Mike Fallon, Fr Kenneth Owens, Antony and Marguerite Kramers, Grace Lee (photocopier supreme), Professor Joe Selling, Professor Herwi Rikhof, Fr Rags Hay-Will, Fr Michael Hollings, Dr Seymour

Spencer, Fr Padraig Gleeson, Barbara Phanjoo, Kathy Gilmour, Fr John McMeel, Canon Denis O'Connell, Sr Anne Doherty, Sr Monica Doyle, Peter O'Reilly, Fr Bernard Traynor, Harry and Rosalyn McCusker, Fr Mark Butlin and Sr Christine Anderson.

In addition, I am particularly grateful to the parishioners of St Mary's, Leslie, who have been prayerfully and patiently supportive of a frequently absent parish priest; to Ruth McCurry of Geoffrey Chapman, an incisive editor who provided just the right balance of carrot and stick (or was it stick and stick?): and, above all, to Una Johnston, the most skilful, generous and reliable of typists it is possible to imagine.

CHAPTER ONE

Jack Dominian: An Introduction

In 1988 Cardinal Basil Hume celebrated Mass at the Central Middlesex Hospital in London. During the homily he explained his personal reason for wanting to be present at the celebrations marking Jack Dominian's retirement from the post of Senior Consultant.

It must have been towards the end of the 1950s, or very early in the 1960s, I, as a young monk, schoolmastering, sat and listened to what must have been then a comparatively young doctor, Jack Dominian. He won't remember me, but I remember him and one thing he said has remained with me for the rest of my days. I'm not quite certain how he put it, but my memory is that he threw it out as an *obiter dictum*.

'Human love is the instrument we can use to explore the mystery of love which God is.'

Whether he actually used these words or not, I don't recall, but that he gave me the thought, I do remember, and it changed from that date my understanding of God. It also gave meaning to the kind of thing that used to go on in my restless heart . . . after all, how can we understand the words of St John when he said 'God is Love' unless from our own experience we can get a glimpse of its meaning? Once you have understood that you are well on the way to discovering the secret of happiness and the purpose of living.

. . . So you see a very good reason for my coming here tonight is to say thank you to Jack for contributing something important in my life. I end as I began with a word of gratitude to one sitting at this moment at my feet, but who, unwittingly, at an important moment in my life has been my master.

Three years earlier Adrian Hastings in his seminal *A History of English Christianity: 1920–85* had looked back on the National Pastoral Congress which had met in Liverpool in 1980 as 'a long awaited moment, a sort of culmination of a period which in some ways despite the failure of clerical leadership at almost every level, had been a great one; an age in which Barbara Ward, Kurt Schumacher and Jack Dominian were prophets and teachers, not only for the Church, but the Nation'. Of these three he singled out Jack Dominian as perhaps 'the most potent single voice from the radical wing of English Catholicism'.

Both Basil Hume and Adrian Hastings recognized the important part played by Jack Dominian in and beyond the life of the Catholic Church in England in the previous 25 years. It is unlikely that either was aware of what it was that moulded a young Greek immigrant into a creative but orthodox Catholic psychiatrist; and then transformed him into so great a challenge to conservative Catholicism that the Jesuit Peter Milward felt compelled in a letter to *The Tablet* in the 1970s to denounce him as 'the enemy within the fold, against which we should all be on our guard'. The first three chapters of this book seek to chart that transformation and then to examine both his early life and the experiences that radicalized him in the 1960s.

In the early 1960s Jack Dominian published two articles, one 'Family limitation', in May 1961 in *Blackfriars*, the other 'Love in Christian marriage' in August 1962 in the *Catholic Herald*. They were the first of many over thirty years in which he has articulated a coherent Christian vision of sexuality and marriage, and they introduce some of his central themes, familiar now partly because of his own repeated presentation of them over the years, but relatively radical at the time.

In the two articles Dominian asserts that 'Christianity is often coupled in the average man's mind with all the precepts and values that deny the meaning and expression of love', and that 'there are many reasons for this, such as the persistent pessimism of centuries with regard to physical sexuality'.

Dominian himself cannot be accused of pessimism. He stresses that the vocation of the vast majority of the members of the Church lies not in priesthood or religious life but in the sacrament of marriage, which becomes their 'instrument of love, perfection, and sanctity', and which 'must thrive with sex in its midst'. He points out how St Paul draws 'a very close analogy between the intimate union of Christ and his Church, and that of husband and wife in the sexual act' and in both articles he suggests that for a couple sexual intercourse is a 'recurrent act of prayer' — the exact words he will use thirty years later in his book *Passionate and Compassionate Love*.

For the early 1960s, this was rather innovatory and startling. However, a closer analysis of these articles shows that Dominian's thought had not at that time developed to anything like its present position. Indeed, in several key areas, his position then was the exact opposite not only of his present stance but also of opinions he was already voicing by the end of that decade.

One such area was the relative status of consecrated celibacy and marriage. In 'Family limitation' Dominian declared that 'the most perfect way of loving God is the total offering of body, mind and heart in the single state dedicated to the service of God'. This state was an 'extremely meritorious one and has precedence over the married state'.

He was no less traditional in his opinion of the relationship between the procreative and unitive aspects of sexual intercourse. Within marriage the 'primary purpose' of sex was to 'co-operate with Almighty God in bringing forth new life; in this end there can be no radical change'. However, 'unfortunately' children were not always universally received 'as a source of immense joy and satisfaction'; indeed 'for many, and this includes quite a few Catholics, children are a burden, . . . unwelcome intruders in a world where woman is fighting hard to be a man'.

One cause of this sad state of affairs was the advent of artificial contraception, which was 'evil'. 'The governing principle for all birth control methods is the demand for immediate satisfaction and the complete absence of sacrifice.' In contrast the use of the infertile period 'neither offends God by insulting the nature of the sexual act which He designed so lovingly and perfectly, nor the dignity of the human body which is the temple of God'. Moreover, its use, which requires a period of abstinence every month, 'has a positive effect' since 'during this period, two people, who love one another very much, freely and of their own accord, sacrifice and offer their mutual love to God. This is a source of grace as well as the means of bringing them much closer, physically, psychologically and spiritually.' The use of the infertile period 'offers the means by which marital love can grow'; all other methods 'fulfil a selfish satisfaction in, and very often, outside, marriage'.

By 1966 Jack Dominian's views on the relative merits of marriage and religious life, the primary purpose of marriage, the emancipation of women, the morality of contraception, and the benefits for married couples of abstention from sex, were almost totally the opposite of those he articulated in these articles.

In September 1966, four years after the publication of 'Love in Christian marriage', Dominian wrote another article, 'Sexuality and psychology', in the Jesuit journal *The Month*. An analysis of this article reveals a very different Jack Dominian in both content and tone. Indeed, 'Sexuality and psychology', along with 'Vatican II and marriage' (also published in 1966), can perhaps be considered his manifestos, an initial proclamation of many of the major themes which he has developed over the last 28 years, with a particular impact because of his almost prophetic conviction. In theory the article was a response to an attack by Paul Halmos, author of *The Faith of the Counsellors*, at the 1966 National Marriage Guidance Annual Conference when Halmos had claimed that 'psychiatrists, psychotherapists and social case workers supported a sexual morality which was a direct descendant of Christian conservative thinking and had nothing to do with psychology'. In fact it was an attack by Dominian himself on the Catholic Church's attitude to sexuality down the centuries and contained his proposal for a new approach to sexual ethics.

Dominian begins the article by suggesting that the foundation of Halmos's attack is his claim that Christianity's attitude to sex is 'conservative, bad and irrelevant'. He then ponders what Halmos's statement might mean from a Catholic perspective. 'It may mean . . . little or no sexual education with possibly damaging remarks and embarrassing silences when the subject is raised. It may mean an inhibiting, ambiguous or negative parental or scholastic attitude to sexuality. It means that masturbation and contraception are gravely sinful actions at the time of writing. It means that premarital intercourse is sinful with ill-defined but extensive innuendoes about premarital and marital chastity. It means that extramarital sexual relations are wrong and so is divorce and remarriage.'

If this is the Catholic attitude to sexuality, Dominian seems determined to lead the assault on it. Certainly he recognizes that 'there is an urgent need to re-examine in detail these various aspects of sexual behaviour and differentiate the central and essential truths that have to be preserved from the mass of misleading social, historical and biological accretions'. However, unlike Halmos, Dominian does not think that a negative attitude to sex is intrinsic to Christian thought and practice. Rather he believes it to be the consequence of three factors: 'first and foremost, the lack of knowledge until this century about the motives and mechanisms of functioning in this area; secondly, the tradition of fear and misunderstanding which has very little connection with Christ's teaching, but a great deal to do with human frailties within the Christian tradition; thirdly, the absence of a vital contribution from the laity in a field which above all involves their life and experience.'

Dominian thinks Christianity has a double task if it is to respond to Halmos and its other critics effectively. First, 'it has to return and examine in detail all aspects of sexual behaviour, not against a background of fear and threat best dealt with by prohibitions and warning, but in the light of Genesis 1:31: "And God saw everything that he had made and behold it was very good." ' To do so, it must 'identify itself afresh with the beauty and goodness of sexuality which were in the Creator's mind' since 'the absence of a whole-hearted acceptance and support of such an approach to sexuality is one of the main accusations against Christianity'. In this area Christian tradition has at times been 'abysmally shortsighted'.

An alteration in the Christian approach to sex would not in his opinion involve innovating change — rather 'it simply means rediscovering what is the norm in the Creator's mind and expressing it in suitable contemporary terms'. That involves accepting the body as good, sexual pleasure as a rich and vitalizing experience, 'and the relationship of the sexes as a harmonising and powerful expression of love and life'.

Secondly, after restoring 'the right values and the appropriate meaning to sexuality', Christianity must try to understand the meaning of disordered sexuality in the light of modern psychological advances. For this to happen, Christian scepticism about psychiatry will need to be challenged and it will be necessary to go beyond a mere blind acceptance of Christian teaching to the reasons behind it. 'The blind obedience which has been prevailing hitherto is no longer sufficient, and part of the contemporary loss in which Christianity finds itself is that humanity is asking questions for which Christianity should have had contemporary answers, but has not.'

This blind obedience in the past has gone hand in hand with ignorance and silence. Dominian recognizes a need for sex-education to be given by parents, since their 'sexual life is the prototype on which the child will base its own future conduct'. They must 'take the child into their confidence and create an atmosphere of mutual trust within which the body will be acknowledged, understood and respected for what it is, an instrument through which communication of love can be achieved'.

Dominian then presents what he believes to be the issue at the heart of this particular debate: the conflict between Christianity's traditional views of sexuality and the contemporary humanist approach. He asserts that 'Sexual pleasure for Christians has been conceived in terms of danger to be guarded against primarily by restricting it to procreative purposes' while for humanists it has been viewed 'as an elysium to be enjoyed to its maximum capacity'. Both see it in terms of quantitative pleasure, 'one side encouraging the maximum amount, the other fearful, circumspecting it with warnings of procreation'. Both fail to realize that 'physical sexual pleasure is an instrument which brings about a communion in which two people, a man and a woman, acknowledge, invite and accept each other as objects of love'. In doing so they reaffirm and reassure in each other feelings of being wanted and loved, 'experiences which we have all had in the hands of our parents and seek again and again from those with whom a relationship of love is sought'. Sexual pleasure cannot be isolated from the human need for closeness: 'sex therefore lies primarily in the service of union and communion, removing isolation.'

This view of sexuality as primarily the means of forging a relationship — within which instinctual gratification will have a prominent place — Dominian believes to be the same as the one present in the 'first historical account we have about the man–woman relationship — Genesis 2:18'. This account contains the 'first clear indication of God's intent', that the man–woman relationship should be 'an instrument of closeness'. However, if this shift in approach is to take place there will need to be 'a massive re-evaluation of the morality of orgiastic experience, heterosexual or homosexual, removing the emphasis from physical pleasure to those characteristics which either enhance or damage the intactness of a relationship of love'. Moreover, when sexuality 'is seen in the capacity to foster affective relationships, then we can enter into the field of psychiatry and psychology, which is very much concerned with understanding those characteristics and traits of the human personality responsible for affective relationships'.

Western society, in Dominian's opinion, has based so much of its concept of the human being on reason and the will that it has failed until recently 'to recognise that the implementation of either requires a minimum of emotional freedom'. Such freedom is dependent on the experience of 'having felt recognised, acknowledged, wanted and accepted first as a person and secondly as a good and lovable person'. He believes that Christianity desperately needs to address this question of freedom and motivation in the area of sexuality — and to do so without immediately taking up a negative and critical stance.

Dominian concludes his manifesto with the statement that ' "God made Man" has given the prototype of the fullness of human intactness'. The task of Christianity is to preach this fact and to help to bring such fullness about. 'This needs action. Action today means research, scientific study with the appropriate tools.' He believes that what Christians require is an institute of sexology and the family, and that such a body will help Christianity 'to repair its most glaring inconsistency: the advocacy of intactness without the means to achieve it. By offering this, Christianity will not be concerned with stigmatising, but with healing.' This call to healing should become the basis for a crusade 'because the poor of the future will not be the homeless and the starving, but the materially affluent who are emotionally and psychologically inadequate'.

The vision presented in this article was not very different from what was implicit in Dominian's earlier articles, with that sense of the goodness and potential sanctity of human love which had already so influenced the young Basil Hume. However, in 'Sexuality and psychology' Dominian clearly articulated themes to which he has returned again and again for over a quarter of a century: the danger that Christianity and Catholicism will not be in touch with the reality of people's experience in the area of sexuality, partly because of their failure to be open to a contribution from the laity; the need to engage in a dialogue with psychiatry and psychology and so to redefine their whole approach, particularly in the area of disordered sexuality; a vision of wholeness as the Gospel goal to which all human beings must aspire, with sexuality as an essential element in those relationships of love which are the normal route to such wholeness; and the necessity of action in the form of scientific research so that Christianity offers not just an ideal but the means to attain it.

Dominian's public articulation of his views was important. But as significant as the actual views was the tone in which he presented them. His visible frustration and anger gave his message a new urgency and cutting edge. It was this combination of righteous indignation and a coherent radical vision which, after the watershed of *Humanae Vitae*, would propel him towards prophetic status in the eyes of many progressive English Catholics. However, Dominian was not dependent on the opinions of others; by the mid-1960s he was already beginning to consider himself a prophet with a mission — the consequence of his diverse experiences since his arrival in England in 1945.

CHAPTER TWO

The early Jack Dominian: 1926–1961

The two major formative influences on Jack Dominian have been his mother Mary and his wife Edith. Apart from National Service and his years at Cambridge, he has lived with one or other of them throughout his life — indeed, for the ten years between 1955 and 1965, with them both. It was because of the influence of his mother that he decided to become a psychiatrist, and because of the influence of his wife that he specialized in marriage and marital pathology; and it was the faith that his parents and his wife communicated to and shared with him that led him to approach psychiatry in general, and marriage in particular, from a deeply Christian perspective.

Jacob Dominian was born on 25 August 1929 in Athens, the third child of an Armenian Catholic father and a Greek Orthodox mother. On one level, his early upbringing was characteristic of a conventional lower middle-class Greek family. His father, Charles, was chief cashier in a bank in Athens, charming, quiet, easy-going and an ardent philatelist. However, it was his mother Mary, a demanding and powerful woman of immense energy and intelligence, who dominated the family, and ensured Jack's childhood was a distinctive one.

An element of mystery and confusion surrounds certain aspects of Mary Dominian's life. Only after her death did her children discover that she had been married to a rich elderly man — and widowed — before she met and married Charles Dominian. They married, and had two children, Leon and Renée, in the first three years of their marriage, and that seemed that, until ten years later when Mary, aged 43, was diagnosed as having a tumour. The doctors were about to operate when it was realized that she was in fact pregnant. If her somewhat confused recollections to her daughter-in-law in her later years are accurate, this pregnancy lasted eleven months and culminated in the birth of Jack and a stillborn twin. Edith Dominian, seeking to separate fact from fantasy, thinks this might well actually have been true; that a foetus had died in Mary's womb just as Jack was conceived, that no miscarriage took place, and that eleven months after the original conception Jack and the stillborn foetus were born together.

Jack Dominian believes that his choice of profession — from the age of sixteen he wanted to be a psychiatrist — was the direct result of his childhood experiences and his relationship with his mother. He paints a picture of a tornado compelled by the social climate of the day to remain a frustrated housewife, and to focus her immense energy on her family. In practice that, from the time he was five, meant Jack. In 1934 his elder brother Leon left for England to live with a maternal uncle who had moved from Athens to Stamford just after the end of the First World War; around the same time his sister Renée was sent off to a convent boarding school, while he remembers his father as a coherent but largely absent force in every-day family life.

The result was a smotheringly repressive and very tense childhood which made Jack sensitive, from an early age, to the complexities of interpersonal relationships and gave him the desire to understand why and how people behave as they do. He believes that the central place that love has in his own thinking springs in part from this early experience of being 'serviced' rather than loved.

This claustrophobic home life meant that the advent of the Second World War was, for Jack at least, a liberating experience. Charles Dominian had been born in Malta, and possessed a British passport. When the Germans invaded Greece in 1941, the family were forced to flee, first to Egypt for six weeks and then to Bombay in India, where they settled for the remainder of the war. In Bombay Jack learnt to speak English, at St Mary's College, where he was also considerably influenced by the incisive minds of the Spanish Jesuits who taught him.

In 1945, at the end of the war, the Dominians moved to England, to Stamford, where they were reunited with Jack's elder brother Leon, and his uncle. The uncle soon found a job for Charles Dominian as an accountant and cashier in a small building firm, while Jack completed the last three years of his secondary education at Stamford Grammar School.

Charles Dominian was a devout Catholic. Jack inherited from

him a similar depth of commitment and faith and was deeply religious from an early age. The influence of Catholicism on him was
accentuated by the disruptions of his childhood, which meant that
the Church was one of the few elements of continuity and security.
It was no surprise, therefore, that it continued to play a large part
in his life after his arrival in Stamford and that he was affected by
the distinctive nature of the English Catholic Church of the 1940s
and 1950s.

This Church was newly respectable and confident, but still largely
self-contained and inward-looking. In a talk Dominian gave in
1968, he looked back on the foundations on which his generation
of Catholics were nurtured.

> The spiritual life rotated around the Mass and the sacra-
> ments, of which the Holy Eucharist and Penance played a pro-
> minent part. Mass in Latin delighted the intellectual few who
> comprehended it and gave much satisfaction to the many
> whose ears and eyes were all attuned to the familiar sounds and
> rituals. Placed in the middle of the Mass was the regular Sun-
> day sermon which occasionally involved commentaries on
> scriptural passages, more often concerned morals and ethics,
> and sometimes an intensive diatribe against such familiar sub-
> jects as birth control, divorce, mixed marriages, sex, psycho-
> logy and Protestants. Morals were set in a legalistic framework
> of evil measured quantitively, negation and prohibition pre-
> dominated and met the needs of behaviour regulated by fear
> and punishment.
> . . . Within this community, we had security and the cer-
> tainty that the Church of Rome neither changed nor erred.
> There was always someone from the local priest through the
> various higher echelons of the hierarchy, right through to the
> Holy Father, who had an answer and the right one at that.
> Doubt and uncertainty were close to heresy, if not in strict
> theology, certainly in the minds of those who entertained them
> and in several of their spiritual advisers.

Dominian 'lived in and loved' this Church which gave 'peace and
spiritual satisfaction' to many. Even from the vantage-point of 1968,
he recognized that 'its priests and bishops were good, dedicated
men trying to serve Christ to the best of their ability, according to
the traditions and customs of the day'. However, 'over one matter
and one matter alone' Dominian came into conflict with it. The

Catholic Church of the 1940s and 1950s had a very negative attitude to the human sciences. Just after his arrival in England Dominian went on a retreat in Birmingham and confided to a Jesuit that he hoped to become a psychiatrist. The Jesuit assured him that there was no surer way to lose his soul. Even today, the recollection of that encounter makes him angry.

That retort, and the opposition he faced from other priests, served to strengthen rather than diminish his ambition. He had no particular interest in medicine, or aptitude for such subjects as chemistry and biology, but he recognized that to become a psychiatrist he needed to qualify first as a doctor. In 1949, after a year's national service, he won a place at Fitzwilliam College, Cambridge, to study medicine. Clerical distrust made him all the more determined to persevere in the long years of relatively uncongenial study that followed.

When Jack Dominian went up to Cambridge he was a loyal and committed Catholic, very traditional in all but his leanings towards psychiatry. Once there, it was natural that he would quickly gravitate towards the Catholic Chaplaincy of Mgr Alfred Gilbey. Soon he was serving Mass and had become an enthusiastic and active member of the Union of Catholic Students. In 1950 at one of their conferences at Spode House in Staffordshire he met Edith Smith, a young student from Newcastle University.

The following year they met again, at another UCS Conference at Worcester. During the proceedings, 70 of the students decided to climb Worcester Beacon to see the sunrise. They set out at half past midnight to walk the eight miles to Malvern, saying the rosary as they did so. While they were climbing the Beacon, Jack decided he was going to marry Edith. Edith, at that time romantically involved with another student back in Newcastle, was more aware of how painful her feet were; but she does at least remember that when Jack linked arms with her to help her up the hill, she had the feeling she could walk to the ends of the earth with him.

In 1952 Jack was on the editorial board of *Crux*, the UCS magazine, while Edith, who had by then broken up with her boyfriend, was UCS national secretary. Jack corresponded with her on UCS matters in characteristically impersonal fashion and then, in November, wrote and asked if he could take her out after the UCS executive meeting they were both due to attend in London. Their romance began in earnest that evening at Lyons Corner House by Marble Arch, faltered in Madame Tussaud's the following morning, but revived in the afternoon at the National Gallery.

In October 1952 Jack finished his pre-clinical training and moved from Cambridge to Exeter College, Oxford. In 1955 he qualified as a doctor and was elected President of the Union of Catholic Students. In the same year he brought an end to three years of hitch-hiking up and down the A1 to Newcastle by marrying Edith Smith.

He is in no doubt that this was the most important event in his life. Edith came from a very loving and stable home. He believes she first brought love into their relationship and has taught him all he knows about love; and he considers his experience of being a husband over 39 years as 'the supreme awareness of my life'.

From 1955 to 1958 Jack did postgraduate work at the Radcliffe Infirmary in Oxford, gaining experience in neurology and geriatrics. His domestic arrangements at the time made him very conscious of the contrasting nature of his relationships with his mother and his wife. His uncle and his brother, who had been responsible for Jack's parents' move to England and Stamford, had emigrated to Rhodesia in 1949. In 1954 Charles Dominian was forced by ill-health to retire from work before he had earned the right to a pension. He and Mary Dominian could no longer afford a home of their own and since their daughter Renée had a very strained relationship with her mother, Jack, as the youngest, felt he should take on the responsibility of looking after his parents. As a result, when Edith and Jack set up home together in Oxford, his parents moved in with them. Charles Dominian died in 1960, but Mary Dominian lived with them until 1965, when she set off first for Rhodesia, and then for Greece.

In 1958 Jack obtained his MRCP from Edinburgh and the extended family, now including two daughters, Suzanne and Louise, moved to Purley in Surrey. By 1964 two more daughters, Elsie and Catherine, had been born. Looking back, their father contrasts that 'supreme awareness' of himself as a husband with his comparative lack of interest in his role as a father. He believes the parenting in the house was done largely by Edith, although he was there in a supportive capacity. Edith thinks he was more involved than this would suggest, but certainly his writings are noticeably more concerned with the relationship between husband and wife than with that between parent and child.

From their home in Purley Jack finally began his psychiatric studies in earnest at the Institute of Psychiatry at the Maudsley Hospital in London. The major influences on him were the neo-Freudians, especially Bowlby, Winnicott, Horney, Erikson and Fromm. These early analysts and psychologists had in the 1940s and 1950s developed the object-relations theory in opposition to the Freudian idea that a child is born with two basic instincts, sexuality and aggression. They claimed, rather, that from its earliest days a child reacts to its parents as persons and therefore that what happens to the personality is determined not by instinctive drives but by interpersonal relations.

These years between 1958 and 1961 were years of creative synthesis. What Dominian was learning about psychosocial development — that the growth of human beings is directly linked to the love they receive — exactly reflected what he was experiencing in his relationship with Edith. It further connected with his theological reading and his growing perception of the Trinity as three persons relating in and through love with each other to culminate in the insight that so struck Basil Hume — that human love was a reflection of divine love and a way of understanding and experiencing it.

In the early 1960s these diverse influences began to bear fruit. In 1961, the year he was awarded a Diploma in Psychological Medicine, Dominian wrote 'Family limitation' for *Blackfriars* magazine. In August 1962 'Love in Christian marriage' appeared in the *Catholic Herald*, and soon after that his first book, *Psychiatry and the Christian*, was published.

In general, *Psychiatry and the Christian* was very favourably received. *The Tablet* stated that 'readers already acquainted with Dr Dominian's articles will come to this book confident of finding the same technical mastery of the subject, combined with a deeply Christian conviction of the human personality'. From across the Atlantic the Jesuit journal *America* observed that it was obvious that 'the author's psychiatric education was on a high plane — as would be expected of a man trained by Sir Aubrey Lewis', and that he was 'apparently equally fortunate in his religious preparation'. However Dominian did not escape entirely from the suspicion of psychiatrists that Catholics of that era tended to have, as Dom Oswald Sumner's comments on the book in the *Downside Review* indicated: 'There will be a special interest in the discussion of responsibility, as it is often thought that it is the aim of various schools of psychotherapy to enable people to sin happily without scruple or feelings of guilt.' Jack Dominian's increasingly angry reaction to such ignorance and prejudice was an important factor in the transformation of his attitude to the Church during the 1960s.

CHAPTER THREE

The radicalization of Jack Dominian:
1961–1969

In 1958, soon after Jack Dominian began his psychiatric studies at the Maudsley Hospital, Professor John Marshall, a neurologist and fellow Catholic, introduced him to Maurice O'Leary, the Chairman of the Catholic Marriage Advisory Council (CMAC). Fr O'Leary invited Dominian to become one of CMAC's medical advisers and counsellors and he accepted. When he first sat down in his chair in the CMAC headquarters in London he was, despite the diversity of his childhood in Athens and Bombay, a not untypical product of the English Catholic Church of the 1940s and 1950s.

In 1958 the morale of that Church had never been higher. In the first half of the twentieth century and especially from 1920 onwards, the Catholic Church had grown continuously, while all the other major churches in England had declined. Although the Church in France and elsewhere might have grave pastoral problems, in England its outlook seemed almost wholly rosy. When the First World War ended it was still a largely working-class institution, but between the wars it had rapidly developed a sizeable middle class and, as Adrian Hastings put it, by 1950 'the steady growth in the number of priests, churches, Catholic schools, convents, the flow of distinguished converts, the nation's increasingly tolerant acceptance of a large Catholic presence and of Catholic educational claims, combined to give Catholicism a very great confidence, a sense of having the ball at its feet, of being irresistibly set upon the upward path'.[1]

Success and acceptance accelerated in the 1950s, a decade which began when the young Dominian, aged 21, was at Cambridge. Poles, Ukrainians, other Eastern European Catholics and a new wave of Irish immigration ensured a continuing growth in numbers.

At the same time international missionary societies like the White Fathers and religious orders like the Cistercians were establishing new foundations. One uncommitted observer, Beverley Nichols, wrote that 'Rome is building new churches all over Britain and as fast as these churches are built, they are filled . . . even if they celebrate a dozen Masses a day'.[2] The number of priests, of 'conversions' and of marriages continued to increase. The Catholic Church had become increasingly respected and respectable; its discipline had been retained, its harshness and under-education lost.

The guiding force behind what seemed a considerable pastoral success was a centralized, clericalized and homogeneous leadership. The dominant figure was Cardinal William Godfrey, Rector of the Venerable English College in Rome — known as the 'Venerabile' — from 1929 to 1938, Apostolic Delegate from 1938 to 1954, Archbishop of Liverpool from 1953 to 1956, and Archbishop of Westminster from 1956 until his death in 1963. His obituary in *The Times* remarked that it could undoubtedly be said of the Cardinal that he had never made an imprudent remark — while his own clergy described his years at Westminster as 'The Safe Period'. As Apostolic Delegate, Godfrey transformed the English Hierarchy into a Venerabile clique by appointing a single sort of bishop — secular priests trained at the English College in Rome, under his predecessor Cardinal Hinsley or himself. Four bishops and five archbishops — Griffin, Masterton, Heenan, Grimshaw and Dwyer — appointed in the 1940s and 1950s were Venerabile men.

These bishops and archbishops had all been formed in the same way and shared a similar approach: 'the "Venerabile" spirit was that of a clerical élite, isolated by seven long years in Rome with little personal contact permitted outside the circle of 50 fellow-students. It was a regime of strict rules punctuated by Christmas theatricals and long summers playing cricket. It cultivated a polite disdain for Anglicans and continental theology. Rome was adored but Italian seldom learnt. Insularity was as important as ultramontanism.'[3] From the end of the Second World War, the English Catholic Church was controlled by priests moulded by this regime. The style of their leadership was illustrated by the admission made in later years by Cardinal Heenan that when he became Bishop of Leeds in 1951, he assumed he was to do his duty by giving orders and the priests were to do theirs by carrying them out.

This ecclesiastical rigidity seemed on the surface to be complemented by an intellectual and cultural creativity. Graham Greene and Evelyn Waugh were accepted as the nation's major novelists, while Tolkien's *The Lord of the Rings*, Frederick Copleston's *History of Philosophy* and Ronald Knox's *Enthusiasm* were contrasting examples of intellectual diversity and brilliance. Appearances were, however, deceptive. These authors all belonged to a generation formed well before the Second World War. Admittedly there were some signs of vitality. Frank Sheed's *Theology and Sanity* (1947) was a clear, convincing and non-clerical presentation of Catholic doctrine by a lay person writing for the laity; the Jesuit Clifford Howell's *The Work of Our Redemption* (1953) successfully communicated the thrust of the Continental liturgical revival; and Spode House, where Jack and Edith Dominian first met, developed in the 1950s into an enlightened conference centre under the Dominican Conrad Pepler. But these were exceptions. The Abbot of Downside, Christopher Butler, was forced in 1958 to lament how 'poverty-stricken' English Catholicism was in both biblical studies and dogmatic theology, while Hugh Trevor-Roper, admittedly no friend of the Church, felt able to pour scorn on 'the intellectual emptiness of modern English Catholicism'.

But although there was ecclesiastical rigidity and intellectual poverty, there were many signs of real vitality. Lay apostolic movements like the Union of Catholic Students — with Jack and Edith Dominian in the vanguard — and the Young Christian Workers flourished; indeed in the late 1950s, an Englishman, Pat Keegan, became the YCW World President. Another focus of interest was the monastic and especially the contemplative life, with the major catalyst being the publication of *Elected Silence*, the autobiography of the Anglo-American Trappist Thomas Merton. A third area of enthusiasm and energy was devotion to Mary and to the Papacy, linked by the definition of the dogma of the Assumption in 1950. Pilgrimages — to Fatima, Walsingham and elsewhere — the Legion of Mary and the Rosary Crusade were all very popular, while the supremacy of the Pope, both in theory and in practice, was never less questioned: 'monks, Marian devotion and the YCW overlapped quite naturally; they shared . . . a common theology and view of life, but above all the deepest loyalty to the contemporary papacy.'[4]

It was in this Church that Jack Dominian was immersed on his arrival in England in 1945. For all its increasing self-confidence, the English Catholic Church still gained its identity from those practices that separated it from everybody else. As Adrian Hastings recognized, it had remained a law unto itself: 'nuns still wore their

antique habits, their strange distinctive head-veils, minor seminaries
were still filled with hundreds of boys from working-class homes
trained in their teens on Latin and celibacy, Benediction and rosary,
the nine first Fridays, plenary indulgences and the special *toties
quoties* indulgence for All Souls. The pattern of popular and clerical
piety remained utterly remote from that of most other Christians
in Britain.'[5] Jack Dominian too was aware in retrospect that
although society had 'certainly respected the holiness of individual
Catholics, the work of priests and nuns, and admired the work of
religious communities', more likely than not it 'knew the Church
if at all, by its teaching on birth control, abstinence on Friday, Sunday Mass and our strict opposition to all other denominations with
whom fraternisation was strictly discouraged'.

The self-contained nature of the English Catholic Church of the
late 1950s and the kind of authority exerted by its leaders make it
easier to understand the assumptions about marriage that Jack
Dominian brought with him when he began to counsel for CMAC.
He had been conditioned by traditional Catholicism to believe that
if a couple didn't sleep together before their marriage, had a
Catholic wedding, went to church regularly, didn't use contraceptives and remained faithful to each other, then, by definition, their
marriage should work. Now he found himself week after week seeing
people who had done all these things and whose marriages were
breaking up.

In 1968 Dominian wrote an article called 'The Christian response
to marital breakdown' in which he pondered what the Christian response was to a situation when between 8 and 12 per cent of married
couples had their marriages dissolved: 'the brief answer is that until
now the theology of marriage has not offered a framework which
could examine such divorces in any terms other than those of
absolute wrongness and sin, with an embroidery of wickedness that
individuals may add to the stark statement.' He went on to describe
how in 1958 he had been 'plunged into this world of absolute sin
in the practice and behaviour of thousands of my patients, and hundreds of my clients in the Catholic Marriage Advisory Council'.
Faced by this he had turned to the teaching of the Church 'to seek
the truth'. However, 'slowly, extremely slowly, it dawned on me
that the principles guiding this teaching, often sincere and honest
as they were, were grasping the truth partially and inadequately,
and therefore pastoral and clinical practice lacked reality, and above
all, in the Church of love, compassion'.

This realization led to what Jack Dominian has described as the 'first and deepest crisis' in his life. The reaction of individual priests to his intended career had meant he was very conscious there were human limitations in the Church in which he had grown up. But what he now perceived as the defective nature of Church teaching on marriage and marital breakdown was an altogether more serious problem. As the 1960s went on, he became increasingly aware of the suffering caused by the Church's teaching and pastoral approach. 'It was my first indisputable realisation that things were not as they were presented — and that really the institutional Church did not have all the answers.' This was 'a staggering realisation for a traditional Catholic'.

Dominian's response to this crisis was twofold. Intellectually he began to move away from the idea of marriage as a contract, and instead to see it as a relationship. This became the foundation on which his whole subsequent understanding of marriage and vision for Christian marriage developed. On a more personal level, his attitude to the Church and to Church authority began to change. 'Because I was faced with the miracle of the cosmos, the miracle of the human being, the miracle of Jesus and the scriptures, and the miracle of love, my intellectual faith, my cerebral faith never really wavered; but my intuitive faith was knocked for six, and my childlike trust in the Church disappeared.'

Just as Jack Dominian was beginning to believe that there might be major defects in the teaching of the Church he loved, so that Church began a process of self-examination. In 1959 the elderly Pope John XXIII, looked upon by most commentators as a caretaker Pope, announced, to general surprise and some consternation, that he was calling a general Council of the Church. The Second Vatican Council — composed of bishops from all over the world — met in Rome between 1962 and 1965.

Its outcome was extremely radical. Adrian Hastings thinks that it was 'the most important ecclesiastical event of this century, not just for Roman Catholics but for all Christians'. This was because 'it so greatly changed the character of by far the largest communion of Christendom that no one has been left unaffected . . . whether it was on the subject of religious freedom, or the action of the Church in the modern world or the appropriate independence of a local Church, or the duty of planned parenthood, the Council took up positions which were not always worked out in their full implications, but which all the same were pregnant with significance for the future . . . the Roman communion, despite occasionally liberal glimmerings, had moved for centuries with great consistency in a single direction. Now for the first time, and in all sorts of ways, that direction had been suddenly and almost solemnly reversed.'[6]

The most significant of these developments was the new orientation the Council gave to theology as a whole. Pope John XXIII had set this in motion with his opening address. 'It is one thing to have the substance of the ancient doctrine of the deposit of faith, but quite another to formulate and reclothe it; and it is this that must — if need be with patience — be held of great importance, measuring everything according to the forms and proportions of a teaching preeminently pastoral in character.' This reformulation must be done 'in accordance with the methods of research and literary formulation familiar to modern thought'.

The Council produced sixteen documents — decrees or 'constitutions' — each known by its opening Latin words. The final decree *Gaudium et Spes* — the Pastoral Constitution on the Church in the Modern World — completed what Pope John had begun. Its opening sentence illustrated its central theme.

> The joy and hope, the grief and anguish of the men of our
> time, especially of those who are poor or afflicted in any way,
> are the joy and the hope, the grief and the anguish of the
> followers of Christ as well. (GS 1)

Gaudium et Spes proposed that the Church should no longer be a Church set apart from the world within an institutional Christendom. Rather it should be characterized by a profound engagement with the reality of the world's experience, entering into solidarity with the experiences of human society and taking humanity seriously in the unfolding of its history.

This new location of the Church's identity meant a new location for theology, and a re-evaluation of what was to count as proper theological activity. Human history mattered; so did human experience. This experience and especially the experience of living the Christian life in the world was to become one of the starting points for theological reflection. In the opinion of the German Jesuit Karl Rahner, *Gaudium et Spes* 'prescribed for theology, the acquisition of a kind of knowledge essential to her activity, which however does not spring from divine revelation but . . . is won from a secular experience, scientifically and systematically gained through modern history, sociology, scientific psychology and futurology'. Tongue in cheek, he added that for the Church this was 'a totally new kind of profane experience, previously non-existent and loaded with all the dangerous, dubious and provisional qualities which are associated with strange scientific empirical manipulation'.[7]

More straightforwardly, the French Dominican Yves Congar declared his belief that at the Council the 'pastors entered the sphere on the one hand of human information and assessment and on the other of induction. This presupposes that they had first accepted the facts as facts, and that they also accepted that the praxis of Christians was to some extent the source of doctrine.'[8] It followed for him that the critical secular disciplines — including psychiatry — were to be in the vanguard of post-conciliar theology.

Moral theology was the branch of theology most affected by this new orientation — and the one in greatest need of renewal. In 1954 the French theologian Aubert, in a survey of the state of Catholic theology at that time, had described it as 'the most decrepit of the ecclesiastical sciences'.[9] The Council duly began the process of reform. *Gaudium et Spes* 33 illustrated an important change in outlook when it declared: 'The Church safeguards the deposit of God's word from which religious and moral principles are drawn. But it does not always have a ready answer to individual questions, and it wishes to combine the light of revelation with the experience of everyone in order to illuminate the road on which humanity has recently set out.'

One subject about which the Council made important statements was marriage. Canon Law reflected much preconciliar theology in dividing marriage into primary and secondary 'ends': the primary end was 'the procreation and upbringing of children', the secondary ones 'mutual help and the remedying of concupiscence'. Jack Dominian was not alone in finding this unsatisfactory. The Council Fathers in debate expressed how inadequate they felt this was and refused to see it merely in terms of a legal contract in which human love was irrelevant. Instead, in *Gaudium et Spes* they developed a theology of marriage as 'a community of love open to life established in covenant between free and equal partners, and founded on the covenant relationship between Christ and his Church'. This approach, as the Irish theologian Enda McDonagh stated recently, was 'scriptural, sacramental and deeply human . . . an excellent expression of a theology of marriage . . . which has by and large stood the test of time since'.[10]

Pope Paul VI, who had succeeded Pope John XXIII on the

latter's death, had removed the controversial issue of contraception
— along with celibacy — from discussion. Paradoxically this decision seemed to give the bishops increased freedom when they came
to debate the question of the transmission of life within marriage.
Gaudium et Spes 50 and 51 shows a new sensitivity to the pressures
on families to limit or postpone further children without violating
the objective moral laws. One analysis of the Council documents
cited this commendation of responsible parenthood as one of the
eight key texts which 'could not have been imaginable as appearing
in a pre-conciliar Roman document'.[11]

From a Catholic perspective the Second Vatican Council was so
unexpected and revolutionary that it is easy to ignore the context
in which it occurred — the cultural and intellectual ferment of
the early 1960s. This ferment was wide-ranging enough for the
Anglican church historian Edward Norman, looking back in 1991
at the reforms of the last two decades in the Catholic Church, to
suggest that while they were 'stimulated and regulated by the
atmosphere of the Vatican Council', nevertheless these reforms
were 'likely to have occurred even if it had not been assembled'.[12]
Certainly throughout the Western world in the early 1960s there was
a sense of a crisis of the total culture affecting many secular institutions as radically as it affected the Church. It was a time of intense
modernization when the relevance and potential for survival of longstanding patterns of thought was seriously questioned.

The 1950s had been years of growing prosperity and freedom —
but of a conservative and limited type. The secular hopefulness of
the early 1960s grew out of this spirit. Events in Britain reflected
what was happening elsewhere. Initially there was great optimism,
an alliance between establishment hopefulness and populist hopefulness. The granting of independence to so many former colonies
helped towards a sense of international progress while contributing
to British euphoria, aided by a continuous and fast rise in the standard of living. Affluence took visible form in the shape of more cars,
more televisions, more washing machines and more holidays for
more people. Universities were founded, prisons were modernized,
and many new hospitals were built. There was a feeling 'that Britain
had dismantled the Empire, but was the better for it, had in fact
never had it so good, that you could lose power but still retain
supremacy in the arts of peace, that you could even combine the
advantages of an old Etonian cabinet with populist culture'.[13]

The mid-1960s saw a subtle but definite shift in mood. Placid prosperity gave way to something more frantic. In 1963 Harold Wilson, about to become Prime Minister, declared: 'We are living in a jet age, but we are governed by an Edwardian establishment mentality'; this, he recommended, should be discarded 'in a break-through to an exciting and wonderful period'. It was in this atmos-phere that *Private Eye* and James Bond first made their appearances, and there was a new media preoccupation 'with youth, with radical-ism, with sex, with a gushing populist turn-about which would somehow sweep away the grouse-moor image of British government and replace it with a glorious combination of Beatle and egg-head Hungarian economist'.[14] The Beatles, indeed, were the symbols of this new mood, and were in their cheerful way completely dismissive of the structured world of class, church, and institutions of any kind.

The five years that followed witnessed increasingly rapid change. In 1965, for example, the death penalty for murder was abolished, the Race Relations Act was passed, and the decision was taken not to create any more hereditary peerages. Values were being trans-formed at the same time as the country was being modernized. The Church in particular found it difficult to respond effectively to these changes. More than any other institution it was vulnerable to the twin thrust of sexual permissiveness and sexual equality while at a deeper level facing an even more serious challenge, the massive shift from religion to secularism as the ruling orthodoxy.

In 1964 John Braine wrote a novel, *The Jealous God*, about Yorkshire Catholics. The main theme of the book was very topical: a sexual crisis as catalyst for the crumbling beliefs of the intelligent young history master at the local Catholic grammar school. Changes in society were already having a dramatic effect on the everyday life of Catholics. The same was not yet true of changes within the Church. There was no mention of the Vatican Council or anything connected with it in *The Jealous God* although in 1964 the Council had already been meeting for two years. Instead, the drama of the novel was played out against a backcloth of 1950s Catholicism — the safe period, Confession and fear of hell all featuring prominently.

The English Catholic Church was not prepared for the Council. Its bishops had been taken by surprise when it was announced. Even as it assembled all that they expected was a reassertion of traditional Catholic values; in the domain of marriage, for example, they assumed it would merely 'reassure and comfort those bewildered by current attacks on the traditional teaching' — which was 'the plain teaching of Christ' who 'calls for sacrifice and self-denial'.[15] As a result, they faced major personal difficulties in coming to terms with its radical nature, and were able to do little to prepare their dioceses for its decrees. In consequence, the Council's initial impact in England was limited.

However, as 1965 and 1966 progressed, an increasing number of progressive Catholics became aware of the Council's revolutionary orientation. Tom Burns, the liberal heir-apparent to Douglas Woodruff, the conservative editor of *The Tablet*, illustrated this growing consciousnes in an internal memorandum.

> The Church has come to a new self-consciousness — a fresh view of her nature, purpose and appropriate manner of life. Whereas it has been the common view hitherto that a human being makes an act of faith in the Church for a solution to his problems, the Church now makes an act of faith in her own people for the fulfilment of her mission. Human intelligence and conscience are now to be trusted with a wider range of apostolate of word and deed not necessarily dependent on the ecclesiastical status quo.[16]

There were some hopeful signs in these years that a potentially fruitful alliance of bishops, theologians and laity would unite for the reform of English Catholicism. The emergence of CAFOD (The Catholic Fund for Overseas Development) and the founding of CIIR (The Catholic Institute for International Relations) were indications of this. So, also, were developments in ecumenism; in the spring of 1966 the Archbishop of Canterbury, Michael Ramsey, visited Pope Paul VI. Their 'Common Declaration' — and the subsequent 'Malta Report' of the Anglican–Roman Catholic Joint Preparatory Commission — set the decisive note for a new and 'special' relationship between the Roman Catholic and the Anglican Churches.

These ecumenical developments were, in fact, the last highpoints in the brief post-conciliar honeymoon. As 1966 went on, just as ordinary Catholics were beginning to become aware of the new openings, the new respect for other Christians and the greater sense of freedom, so, paradoxically, at another level the atmosphere was becoming more sombre. In December the dramatic departure of the well-known lecturer, author and editor of *The Clergy Review* Charles Davis from both the priesthood and the Church heralded a period of tension and increasing confrontation between the hierarchy and progressive Catholics, lay and clerical.

Jack Dominian was among those lay Catholics who were beginning to adopt a more aggressive tone in public. The Vatican Council had begun its deliberations in 1962 at a critical period in his life. As a consequence, he had watched the Council develop with a mixture of expectation and detachment. At the same time he had sought to develop a new Christian approach to sexuality, based on increased receptivity to the insights of psychology, and he had grappled afresh with the concept of Christian marriage, grounding his vision on the idea of relationship rather than contract. In both, he was more open to the intellectual and cultural ferment of the early 1960s than he would have been had his intuitive faith not been so seriously challenged by his experience as a marriage counsellor. Yet whereas Charles Davis, reacting strongly against the claustrophobic clerical environment in which he had lived since the age of fifteen, had rejected the Church as a whole, declaring that he had not really believed in its biblical and historical claims for some time, Dominian still retained and publicly professed a loyalty and love for the Church. He began to devour the Council documents as soon as they were published and by mid-1966 was ready to speak out in public.

In September 1966 Jack Dominian addressed the CMAC Annual conference on 'Vatican II and marriage'. With his article 'Sexuality and psychology' published that same month in *The Month*, it acted almost as a personal manifesto illustrating the transformation that had taken place in his attitude and approach in the previous four or five years, revealing some of the reasons for the radicalization of his own vision, touching on most of the major issues surrounding marriage that he would continue to return to and analyse in the years ahead, and challenging the Church to change its position in certain key areas. It is worth examining in detail because in few articles before or since has Dominian been so outspoken or so worn his heart on his sleeve.

The address is in two parts, the first entitled 'The nature of the Church', the second longer section headed 'The statement on marriage'. Dominian begins with a quotation from Pope John's opening address at the Council in which he stated that the Church 'must ever look to the present, to the new conditions and new forms of life introduced into the modern world which have opened new avenues to the Catholic apostolate'. Dominian draws the conclusion that 'continuity, renewal, modification and when necessary radical changes thus became the work of the Council'. Then he declares

his intention in the first half of his talk tò examine texts from the
Council documents which he believes to have major implications in
determining the role of a lay organization like CMAC.

Most of these texts are drawn from the Dogmatic Constitution on
the Church — *Lumen Gentium* (The Light of the Nations) — which
has been 'generally hailed as the masterpiece of the Council and the
foundation on which so much of the other declarations depend'.
Dominian cites several passages from it which 'in the strongest possible language' establish 'the significance of the laity in their own right'.
One of them states that although the Pope and bishops are entrusted
with the office of teaching and governing, 'the priestly, prophetic and
kingly roles of Christ belong to all the baptised faithful including . . .
the laity' (LG 31); another emphasizes that 'the prophetic functions
of Christ are not confined to the Hierarchy' (LG 35); while a third
points out that it is Christ's wish that the laity have the 'principal role'
in the spread of the Kingdom (LG 31).

Dominian lays particular stress on what *Lumen Gentium* says about
the laity's relationship with their priests:

> Let sacred pastors recognise and promote the dignity as well
> as the responsibility of the layman in the Church. Let them
> willingly make use of his prudent advice. Let them confidently
> assign duties to him in the services of the Church, allowing
> him freedom and room for action. Further let them encour-
> age the layman so that he may undertake tasks on his own
> initiative. (LG 37)

Ideally, every member of the Church contributes to its well-being,
the laity 'passing on their own personal and inimitable experience
to their pastors, who specially assisted in this way will, in turn, help
the Pope to govern the Church'. Dominian points out that *Lumen
Gentium* states that it is 'the body of the faithful as a whole', who
cannot err in matters of belief — and similarly that it is 'the People
as a whole' who are characterized by 'a supernatural sense of faith'.
This faith 'has an unerring quality', when 'from the bishops down
to the last member of the laity, it shows universal agreement in matters of faith and morals'.

He concludes this positive examination of *Lumen Gentium*'s presentation of the Church's fundamental theological characteristics
with a significant illustration of his changed attitude: 'it will be my
contention that the People of God viewed in this sense cannot be said
to have participated in the pronouncements on birth control and

therefore any reassessment of this topic however radical will be consistent with this pronouncement.'

Dominian believes that *Lumen Gentium* marks a transformation in
the Church's way of presenting itself and of relating to others. 'This
is no longer a triumphant, domineering, polemical, accusatory or
condemning Church. It is a Church which wishes to reaffirm its
desire to serve and love. To non-Catholics, it turns with an earnest
desire to begin the long road back to reunion. It is a penitent Church
acknowledging that men of both sides were to blame.'

He is also appreciative of the Church's new willingness to dialogue
with the non-believer: 'for me, this dialogue is most exciting for I
have long believed that defective as the humanist thinking is in some
respects, it has represented hitherto noteworthy advances in the con-
ceptualisation of man which have been ignored and attacked by
Christianity unjustly.' He cites one passage in which the Church
acknowledges the value of such thinking, as 'one of the most
thoughtful and provocative statements of the whole Council', and
then launches into a *cri de coeur* in which the frustrations and turmoil
of the previous few years are very visible.

> It is one of the agonising experiences of our times to witness
> the Church of God, the Church of Love, having slowly and
> rather pathetically to climb down and learn from others, what
> by its very nature has always been held in its own treasury.
> In particular the Church of love has to learn the contemporary
> mode of loving man from others. What others have developed
> and presented is indeed far from satisfactory, but the handicap
> with which the Church is burdened is that the world will not
> listen to her because she did not listen to the world first. This
> is the first great act of repair which we have to accomplish.

Dominian is not optimistic that this 'act of repair' will take place.

> Having accomplished its own internal renewal in the theology
> of understanding itself, and in its liturgy, there is still the great
> danger that men will pass it by unless it recognises, hails and
> converses with contemporary man meaningfully. The Council
> has made a brave attempt to deal with this problem but there
> can be little doubt in my mind that the depth of the Council's
> examination and understanding of the Church's nature is
> nowhere matched in its understanding of man with the possible
> exception of the declaration on religious freedom.

The second half of the address is a critical appraisal of what the Council says about marriage. The Council Fathers in *Gaudium et Spes* had transformed the Church's theology of marriage in a way that many moral theologians believe still holds good for today. In 1966, however, Jack Dominian felt it was a case of too little, too late. He does recognize 'some very promising and encouraging elements' in the relevant sections of *Gaudium et Spes* but he 'cannot conceal' that overall he found it 'a disappointing document'. He continues: 'I confess, I expected a great deal and my disappointment reflects my concern and belief that this is one of, if not the most important subject facing the Church today which deserves a much fuller treatment.'

Dominian then, somewhat self-righteously, comments on the growing tension in the Church of 1966:

> I am not criticising anyone in particular. One of the favourite pastimes of some Catholics in recent times is to voice a criticism and simultaneously to attack a bishop, a hierarchy or the Pope. I do not find it easy to criticise because as a psychiatrist, I do not see blameworthy responsibility as easily as others do. What is unsatisfactory in the Church is ultimately our collective responsibility. As for the bishops, those who wish to persist with their fantasies in making ogres of them, this is a matter for their conscience. In my own experience they have tried to do their duty to the best of their ability. In the fulness of time, they will be responsible to Almighty God, as we shall all be for our actions. It is possible, however, that Christ will say to the married, and why did you not help them to understand your sacrament?

In 1967 Dominian published his second book *Christian Marriage — The Challenge of Change*, the culmination of the rethinking of his vision of marriage that his counselling experiences and the accompanying crisis had forced upon him. The considerable research and introspection involved was one reason why the Council's statements on marriage seemed to him somewhat superficial. It also helped to explain the resentment he felt at the Council Fathers' failure 'to appreciate the significance of psychology and/or psychiatry', as the insights offered by these disciplines were the basis of his own approach.

This failure is his 'other deep disappointment in the documents of the Council'. Psychology is 'one of the subjects that has revolutionised our thinking about man in the last seventy-five years'. The absence 'of a detailed examination of the subject' during the Council, is 'a profound omission'.

In his subsequent analysis of the reasons for this omission, Dominian shows why he believes it is no longer possible for theology or pastoral practice to ignore psychology.

Man's status has rested so far on his intellect, the freedom of his will and his spiritual capacity to reflect the image of God and thus to become an adopted son of God the Father. The validity of his spiritual state remains unchanged, but his humanity and therefore the image of God will in the future be accurately reflected, only if, to his intellect and will, is added the fulness of his psychological intactness.

The remainder of the address is an examination of the pronouncements on marriage in *Gaudium et Spes* 'in the light of this human intactness'. Dominian cites section 48 in which the indissolubility of marriage is reaffirmed and then contrasts that ideal with the rapidly increasing figures for divorce in England and Wales between 1960 and 1963. He asks whether all these people are breaking God's law and suggests that 'so far we have thought so because we have worked on the belief that in the absence of any of the usual impediments, a man and a woman who freely consent to take each other in marriage are validly married'.

His own experience tells him this is no longer an adequate stance. 'In my work over seven years with the CMAC and in the course of my ordinary psychiatric duties I have become convinced that we shall have to re-examine the criteria of a valid marriage.' Although 'men and women can certainly give and receive each other's verbal vows to take each other in marriage', what in fact has to be established is whether 'they are physically and psychologically capable of effecting a minimum expression of what these vows signify'. Indeed 'one can say with a degree of certainty that some marriages are not marriages despite their apparent fulfilment of all the usual criteria' because 'one or both partners are incapable of giving a minimum expression of their commitment to love their spouse'. This view has become the basis for many of the annulments that are now granted by Church tribunals.

He goes on to cite research which shows that marriages of young people, pre-marital pregnancies and the combination of the two are major contributory factors to marital breakdown. He suggests that the Church needs to recognize the significance of these findings by alerting priests and couples to the inherent dangers of such a situation, and by seriously reconsidering its consent to marriages which

run a high risk of breaking down. These twin recommendations are
dependent on the availability and effectiveness of courses of preparation for marriage. Dominian here stresses the importance of such
courses for the first but by no means the last time.

Dominian is encouraged by the 'strong reaffirmation of married
love' in *Gaudium et Spes* which 'stands in marked contrast to the
previous juridical language of contract, duties and obligations which
have been such a powerful handicap in coming to terms with the
personal elements of marriage in the past'. However, his enthusiasm
is restrained — because his experiences as a marriage counsellor
have made him very critical of what he perceives as the Church's
tendency to mouth platitudes about love without examining what
that love actually means in practice. He thinks that *Gaudium et Spes*
is very guilty of this. It contains a series of statements 'all of which
are perfectly true' but which 'can easily become meaningless exhortations'. He cites examples from the document:

> This love is eminently human love and since it is directed from
> one person to another through an affection of the will it can
> enrich the expressions of body and mind with an unique
> dignity . . . by its generous activity it grows better and grows
> greater . . . it remains steadfastly true in body and in mind in
> bright days or dark . . . the couple will painstakingly cultivate
> and pray for constancy of love, largeheartedness and the spirit
> of sacrifice . . . finally authentic conjugal love will be more
> highly prized, and wholesome public opinion created, regard-
> ing it, if Christian couples give outstanding witness to faithful-
> ness and harmony in that same love. (GS 49)

Dominian accepts that there may appear a note of parody in these
quotations. However, 'another of the great deficiencies of the past
has been to substitute genuine, well-meant and sincere exhortations
for the necessary information and direction in conjugal matters, of
which birth regulation is an outstanding example. This will just not
do anymore, for if Christians turn to the Church in vain they will
turn elsewhere.'

He is convinced that Christianity must concern itself with these
'minute-to-minute experiences of the spouses, for it is here that the
battle for every marriage will be fought'. Marriage is a 'secular
reality' and it is within 'the intactness of this secular reality that the
supernatural order of the sacrament must ultimately rest'. That is
one reason why he is delighted with 'the significant but very brief

reference to sexuality' in *Gaudium et Spes*.

> This love is uniquely expressed and perfected through the marital act. The actions within marriage by which the couple are united intimately and chastely are noble and worthy ones. Expressed in a manner which is truly human, these actions signify and promote that mutual self-giving by which spouses enrich each other with a joyful and a thankful will. (GS 49)

Dominian thinks that the sexual excesses of the 1960s have been related to centuries of Christian pessimism on the subject, and therefore that this 'affirmation of the goodness in all that is essentially physical and psychological in sexuality' is all the more significant and promising. It follows, in his opinion, that the Church will now 'have to pay minute attention to the preparation of married couples in experiencing these exchanges with the maximum possible respect for their physical and psychological content'.

This brings Dominian to what he considers 'the central issue of our day, the matter of birth control'. At the time of his address the Commission set up by Pope Paul VI was coming to the end of its deliberations. Dominian's comments show how much his views had changed since he had written 'Family limitation' and 'Love in Christian marriage', and help to illustrate why *Humanae Vitae*, still two years away from promulgation, provoked the consternation in him that it did.

> Nearly all of us at this conference were brought up to believe that contraception is a grave sin. Few questioned this teaching until the last few years, particularly since the advent of the pill, and the book by John Rock *The Time Has Come* [1963]. The Church then went into a critical examination of this matter and to the great astonishment of all of us it became evident that what appeared to be palpably obvious and morally invincible turned out to be a condemnation which in the final argument could not be sustained by any clear-cut arguments, reason, or support from the scriptures. The best thing that can be said of the present position is that we are looking today for the reasons which we all took for granted. The implications of this discovery for the Church are momentous but for the time being there are bound to be feelings of hurt, anger, a sense of betrayal and mistrust.

He continues by stating publicly for the first time his belief that 'a reformulation of doctrine is necessary' because 'the essence of sexual intercourse is an act of love first and foremost, within which procreation takes place at freely chosen and appropriate moments within marriage'. The morality of contraception 'must be seen in terms of whether any individual contraceptive promotes or inhibits the humanity of the act'. When contraceptives are found 'which do not seriously impair the intactness of the exchange', then 'in my reformulation no intrinsic evil is encountered'. He cites passages in *Lumen Gentium* and in the Decree on Ecumenism which in his opinion allow for such a reformulation.

Dominian acknowledges that the Council's avoidance of the terms 'primary' and 'secondary' for the purposes of marriage is 'a great step forward in the formulation of a marital theology'. However there is a serious defect in the document because 'the proper balance between procreation and the development of the spouses and children as people is no more than mentioned'. He believes that research and experience show that the well-being and growth of the child depends on the well-being and maturity of the parents and therefore that rather than 'praising a large family on the basis of numbers' as *Gaudium et Spes* does, it should be more widely understood that 'no child should be conceived unless its parents want it, are ready to receive it, and can meet its minimum physical, emotional and spiritual needs'.

He proceeds to examine the condemnation of abortion in *Gaudium et Spes* which, in his opinion, lacks pastoral sensitivity: 'here, as elsewhere, . . . there is no hint whatsoever suggesting we know any of the reasons why women wish to have an abortion and how we can help them. One of the greatest deficiencies in the Christian Church has been the contrast between the condemnation of sexual sins and the efforts made to understand and help those involved in these situations.' He believes that 'the woman who has an abortion does wrong' but that 'with rightful justice, she may ask of the Church "And what help did you give me?" ' This giving of help 'is one of the most urgent challenges facing all of us and not only in the matter of abortion but in the whole field of sexual deviations and difficulties'.

Dominian concludes his analysis of the Council documents on a more positive note. He is encouraged that *Gaudium et Spes* has reaffirmed the doctrinal definition that marriage is a sacrament, and has indicated how married love is caught up into divine love 'which is structured on the model of His union with the Church'. This is 'the supreme expression of Catholic theological thought . . . a mature and enriching spiritual fact which is one of the jewels of our Catholic tradition'.

This article, along with 'Sexuality and psychology', presents the Dominian vision, transformed since the early 1960s and now clearly identifiable with what he continues to present and communicate today. It is a vision based on a preferential option for the poor as he believes poverty to be most widely experienced in the Western world, hence the final message he leaves with his audience.

> Every neighbour has a rightful call on our love, but especially the needy and the poor. The poor have been traditionally in the past those in need of food and shelter, work and money. These problems have not been eliminated, but in the advanced nations greatly ameliorated. Here the new poor will be found among the psychologically and socially handicapped of our age. Alcoholism, marital breakdown, sexual deviation, delinquency, suicidal attempts are the acts of the new poor and the new call for the Church and in this work our organisation has a unique role to play and a vital contribution to make.

There were three main reasons for the changes in Jack Dominian's attitude and approach to marriage, sexuality and the Church between those early articles in 1961 and 1962 and his two clarion-calls, 'Sexuality and psychology', and 'Vatican II and marriage' in 1966. The first was his experience as a CMAC counsellor and as a psychiatrist in the ferment of the 1960s which convinced him that Church teaching on marriage, marital breakdown and contraception was out of touch with reality and, therefore, in need of revision. The second was the impact of the Vatican Council, both in the expectations it aroused — especially through what *Lumen Gentium* presented as the role of the laity — and in what Dominian himself experienced as its disappointments, including the generally admired references to marriage in *Gaudium et Spes*. The third was his anger at the Church's general attitude to psychiatry and psychology, anger repressed by him over the years but released by the liberating effect of the Council and its aftermath.

Two later Dominian talks and articles illustrate how closely these three reasons are interconnected. In early 1968, in a talk to the Coventry Newman Society on 'Psychoanalysis and the Christian life', he stated: 'Vatican II has come and gone and the Holy Spirit has made us aware of the enormous gap between spiritual reality and fantasy. Our eyes have been opened to the limitations of our vision.' For all the integrity of preconciliar bishops and priests, 'a great many things which they were trying to do, which we were all trying to do, were irrelevant to the spiritual needs of our time'. Moreover, although 'more than one priest warned me against taking up psychiatry which was considered a danger to my faith, if I retain and nurture my faith today, it is principally through my experience in psychoanalysis which has illuminated the meaning of love more than any other teaching and has complemented the scriptures in a vibrant and significant manner'.

In 1973 Dominian wrote an article entitled 'Birth control and marital love' which is strongly autobiographical. In it he looks back on 'the turbulent period following Vatican II' when 'controversy was marked and persistent' and suggests that there were profound psychological issues at the centre of that conflict.

> Traditional Catholic upbringing has generated an atmosphere of utter conviction that all ordained priests — certainly a bishop, and above all the Holy Father — represent the person of Christ in special ways and disagreement with any of these invested the exchange with the peculiar guilt feeling of offending someone important. Furthermore in the authoritarian structure in which the Church's organisation existed, such guilt was coupled with fear of the consequences, fear which ultimately whispered of hell-fire somewhere in the background and, if not hell-fire, certainly the loss of approval from someone precious. Psychologically the relationship between lay persons and hierarchical structure was a continuation of the parent–child relationship.

All this, in his opinion, changed after Vatican II. 'There was a sudden and pent-up release of these accumulated tensions of centuries and without any shadow of doubt there was open rebellion against the hierarchy, which was a reflection of the repudiation of the young child status vis-à-vis the grown up.'

This inclination to rebellion was not, however, overtly apparent in the Dominian of early 1968. Indeed he struck a distinctly optimistic note during the second half of his talk to the Newman Society. 'Vatican II has introduced English into the Mass, made ecumenism an urgent necessity, reaffirmed the significance of the scriptures, and made us all realise, as the people of God, our collective responsibility in maintaining and extending the kingdom of God. Personal and religious freedom are themes capturing our imagination, sexuality is about to change gear from centuries of pessimism into one of optimism, admittedly a gear hard to find and difficult to place but still grindingly present. All this is exciting, invigorating and very necessary.'

As 1968 progressed this optimism began to disappear, inside and outside the Church. For many English Catholics the turning-point was the replacement of the Latin Mass by Mass in the vernacular. The Latin Mass had been the great symbol of English Catholic identity. Now it all but disappeared, a revolution carried out in a very disciplined fashion, with very little enthusiasm or explanation but with considerable pastoral and ecumenical implications. With its passing, both the special mystery and the unquestioned clericalism of Catholicism began to fade. While Dominian himself and other progressive Catholics generally welcomed this development, for many others it was a deep and sudden shock and involved a sharp loss of identity. Morale suffered and the process of polarization between progressives and conservatives accelerated.

The increasing tension and confrontation within the Church in 1968 was reflected in developments outside it. Change continued at a breathless rate; abortion was legalized as was homosexual behaviour in private between consenting adults. Divorce was made far easier to obtain. Yet the sense of euphoria characteristic of the early and mid-1960s had begun to give way to pessimism.

In the opinion of Adrian Hastings, 1968 was 'the year not just for Britain, but much more for the world as a whole, in which the leftward-looking intelligentsia, the optimistic populist reformism, which had provided the consensus characteristic of the sixties as a decade, came finally and decisively to the moment of truth'.[17] There were student riots in the spring in Paris and elsewhere. Martin Luther King was assassinated in April and Robert Kennedy in June. In August the Russians extinguished Dubček's exciting experiment — 'socialism with a human face' — in Czechoslovakia. In addition there were the horrors of Vietnam and of the Nigerian Civil War, the stormy emergence of the Civil Rights Movement in Northern Ireland and at home Enoch Powell's 'rivers of blood' speech. It was also the year of *Humanae Vitae*.

Pope Paul VI had asked the Vatican Council not to discuss the controversial issues of celibacy and artificial contraception. Instead he had enlarged the commission that Pope John XXIII had set up in 1963 to consider the threat of overpopulation and, since it had become clear that the underlying basic issue was the Church's whole stance on marital sexuality, asked it to reassess the morality of contraception. Meanwhile, the Council had strongly approved responsible family planning, and had recognized moral grounds for limiting the number of children a couple chose to have.

In 1966 Pope Paul had informed the world that his 'broad, varied, and extremely skilled international commission' had presented its findings, but had added that they 'cannot be considered definitive' without consideration of their serious doctrinal and pastoral implications. Even so, expectations of a change in the Church's position were high, and were further increased in April 1967 with the leaking of the Commission's report first in the *National Catholic Reporter* in the USA and then in *The Tablet*. It stated that 'the morality of sexual acts between married people takes its meaning first of all and specifically from the ordering of their actions in a fruitful married life . . . It does not then depend upon the direct fecundity of each and every particular act'; and it advised in favour of a change in official teaching. The International Congress for the Lay Apostolate, meeting the same year, took a similar line.

The Pope had reserved the final decision for himself. As well as the official report, he also had to consider a position paper from four dissenting theologians on the Commission who maintained that contraception was morally evil and argued against any change. However while he agonized over the decision for more than a year, many bishops, Cardinal Heenan among them, prepared their dioceses for the 'development' in the Church's position that they expected him to announce.

Finally, on 25 July 1968, Pope Paul issued his encyclical letter *Humanae Vitae* — 'on the right ordering of propagating human offspring'. In spite of passages expressing pastoral understanding for the difficulties facing married couples, he came down in favour of the arguments of the Commission's four dissenting theologians and re-emphasized traditional teaching.

The Encyclical aroused completely unprecedented reactions both within the Roman Catholic Church and outside it. Philippe Delhaye, one of the members of the Commission, described the immediate aftermath of its appearance as 'the month of theological anger'. In the first few days of August there were five columns of letters on the subject in *The Times*, while in *The Tablet* of 3 August, Tom Burns, entitling his editorial 'Crisis in the Church', sought to lead an 'open rebellion'. Burns declared 'we must honestly confess that neither joy nor hope can we derive from the Encyclical itself'. The real issue, in his opinion, was one of authority. The publication of *Humanae Vitae* had meant that 'a new chapter on the relationship of the Pope with the bishops and with the faithful at large has now opened on a sombre note. There will be doubt and dismay about the Church herself among the more reflective members . . . loyalty to the faith and the whole principle of authority now consists in one thing; to speak out this disillusion of ours, not be silenced by fear. We who are of the household of the faith and can think of no other have the right to question, complain and protest, when conscience impels. We have the right and we have the duty out of love for the brethren.'

The encyclical was published when Jack Dominian was on holiday in the Costa Brava with his family and the family of a Jewish psychiatric colleague from the Central Middlesex Hospital. Edith Dominian recalls how she and Jack were sitting reading on the beach, their backs against a rock, when their friend returned from the nearby village with an English paper. She has a vivid memory of the paper sailing through the air to land on Jack, his frenzied reaction to the headline, and her prolonged and eventually successful efforts to restrain him from returning to England immediately to register his protest.

When the Dominians finally did arrive back in England there were further signs of the 'sudden and pent-up release' of 'the accumulated tensions of centuries'. These culminated in a letter of nonconformity signed by 55 priests in *The Times* of 2 October and a similar dissenting letter from 75 distinguished lay Catholics in *The Tablet* that same week. There were three main targets for the encyclical's critics: the intrinsic force of the arguments from natural law and tradition which were utilized to justify the Pope's conclusion despite the findings of the Papal Commission; the manner in which the Pope had reserved the final judgement and statement to himself; and the binding force of the conclusion on members of the Church. The overall effect was 'not only immediate confusion, but an immense and lasting decline in ecclesiastical morale. The whole situation was demoralising.'[18]

Any doubts that Jack Dominian had about whether he was right to challenge the Church in its teaching on sexuality and marriage were dispelled by *Humanae Vitae*. During the 1960s he had developed an almost prophetic zeal; *Humanae Vitae* confirmed his sense of mission. In addition it was directly responsible for giving him the third and most important of his three public platforms.

Dominian believes that three men have made it possible for him to communicate his vision of sexuality and marriage to the wider world. The first was Maurice O'Leary, who as Chairman of CMAC gave him total freedom within the organization for 20 years. The second was John Todd of the publishers Darton, Longman & Todd, who was willing to publish any book Dominian wrote between 1967 (*Christian Marriage*) and 1991 (*Passionate and Compassionate Love*). The third was Tom Burns, editor of *The Tablet* between 1968 and 1982.

The Tablet had immediately opposed *Humanae Vitae*. To do so effectively, however, Tom Burns realized that he needed to be able to present an alternative and authoritative vision to that offered by the official Church in the encyclical. In the 'Notebook' of *The Tablet* of 20 September 1969 he introduced 'the first in a series of four articles on Christian Marriage by Dr Jack Dominian', declaring that it honoured a promise made by Dominian to him over a year before. In the years that followed, Burns allowed Dominian to write on whatever subject he chose, giving him what Dominian considered a 'prestigious and worldwide' platform, and one that was directly responsible for enabling him to become 'perhaps the most potent single voice' from the more radical wing of English Catholicism.

Notes

1 A. Hastings, *A History of English Christianity 1920–85* (London: Collins, 1986), p. 644.
2 B. Nichols, *A Pilgrim's Progress*, p. 218; quoted in Hastings, *History*, p. 563.
3 Hastings, *History*, p. 479.
4 Ibid., p. 483.
5 Ibid., p. 490.
6 Ibid., p. 528.
7 Karl Rahner, *Foundations of Christian Faith*; quoted in J. McDade, 'Catholic theology in the post-conciliar period' in A. Hastings (ed.), *Modern Catholicism* (New York: Oxford University Press, 1991), p. 400.
8 Y. Congar, 'A last look at the Council' in A. Stacpoole (ed.), *Vatican II by Those Who Were There* (London: Geoffrey Chapman, 1986), p. 348.
9 R. Aubert, *La Théologie Catholique au milieu de XXe siècle* (Paris, 1954), pp. 7–8; quoted in J. Mahoney, *The Making of Moral Theology* (Oxford: Clarendon Press, 1990), p. 302.
10 E. McDonagh, 'The conciliar documents' in Hastings (ed.), p. 104.
11 A. Hastings, 'The key texts', ibid., p. 60.
12 E. Norman, 'An outsider's evaluation', ibid., p. 460.
13 Hastings, *History*, p. 509.
14 Ibid., p. 516.
15 L. Pyle (ed.), *Pope and Pill*; quoted in Mahoney, p. 263.
16 Quoted in M. Walsh, *The Tablet: A Commemorative History 1840–1990* (London: The Tablet Publishing Company, 1990), p. 64.
17 Hastings, *History*, pp. 514–15.
18 Ibid., p. 576.

CHAPTER FOUR

Jack Dominian: Basic anthropology and theology

Since 1968 Jack Dominian has been extraordinarily active and pro-
lific. He has published eighteen books, fifteen by himself, one with
the scientist A. R. Peacocke, one with the Anglican bishop Hugh
Montefiore, and most recently *The Everyday God* with Edmund
Flood, a Benedictine monk. He has written over forty articles in
journals ranging from *Theology* and *The Way* to *Health Visitor* and
Vogue; several chapters in multi-author works; and over a hundred
articles and book reviews for *The Tablet*.

In addition Dominian has given more lectures and talks than the
combined total of his articles, book reviews and books. The subjects
range from studies of marriage and marital pathology to examina-
tions of the impact of changes in marriage and sexuality in Western
society on Christian thought and tradition.

From 1968 until his retirement in 1988 he was Senior Consultant
at the Central Middlesex Hospital. In 1971 he founded the Marriage Research Centre and remains its director. For much of that
time he has counselled for CMAC; and he still retains his private
counselling practice.

As the previous chapter has illustrated, major changes took place
in Dominian's thought in the 1960s. Since then his vision has evolved
much more gradually with the occasional new insight or emphasis;
recent articles and talks have tended, for example, to concentrate
on the concept of the 'domestic Church'. In no one book has he
attempted to present a final synthesis of his approach but two of his
most recent works, *Sexual Integrity: The Answer to AIDS* (1987) and
Passionate and Compassionate Love: A Vision for Christian Marriage (1991),
contain, scattered through their pages, the explicit and implicit
anthropological and theological foundations of his approach to

sexuality and the human person. This chapter will seek to bring
them together in a coherent fashion.

Jack Dominian's vision of the human person, as it is articulated
in these two books, is rooted in his belief that each person is a sexual
being in the broadest sense, and that this sexuality is embedded in
each individual from birth rather than something which emerges at
puberty. Dominian accepts the Freudian view that instinctive drives
play an important part in the development of the personality, but
he does not think that they determine it. In his opinion, these drives
are normally integrated in the whole person in the process of loving
relationships, first with mother, then with father, and then with
other people. The key to his anthropology is this interplay between
person, relationship and love; he believes we develop as human
beings through our loving relationships.

The first and most important of these relationships is a child's
relationship with its parents: 'the foundations of love are laid
in our childhood and it is to these that we revert when we relax in
the intimacy of a loving relationship. So in order to understand
the nature of our loving expectations, we have to understand these
deep layers of our childhood experiences.' Since a child's dynamic
development largely accounts for the growth of its affective life,
Dominian believes that the main insights of dynamic psychologists are indispensable in the understanding of the human
person.

Dominian's anthropology is firmly based on the work of three
neo-Freudian dynamic psychologists, Bowlby, Winnicott and
Erikson, so much so that in *Sexual Integrity* and *Passionate and Compassionate Love* it is not always easy to separate Dominian's presentation
of their thought from his personal interpretation of them and his
own particular views. Of the three, John Bowlby has had the
greatest influence on him.

Dominian believes that Bowlby's genius lay in the way he
revealed that the view of bonding generally accepted until the
mid-1950s — as occurring through the reduction of certain drives,
in particular those of food in infancy and sex in adulthood — did
not do justice to human behaviour. Bowlby's work was based on
ethology, and in Dominian's opinion it showed that infants become
attached to their mother within the first weeks of their life, that this
attachment has 'affectional connotations', and indeed that 'attachment behaviour characterises human behaviour from cradle to the
grave'.

The attachment formed between mother and child is based on vision, sound and touch: 'the young infant stabilises the relationship by familiarising itself with the mother's face and gradually the rest of her body: this is the recognition of vision. Concurrently, the young child becomes acquainted with the sound of her voice: this is the recognition of sound. Finally an intimate connection is formed with touch through holding and being held.'

Through these physical means and the sense of smell 'the baby forms an affective attachment; that is to say, it is emotionally bonded to the mother and thereafter wants to stay by her side'. This attachment is then extended to the father 'and other key persons who form a continuous presence' in its life.

'Attachment theory' according to Dominian is a 'major advance on Freudian thought which saw mother's role principally in terms of food provider' and has important ramifications for the understanding of human sexuality. If 'the essential human interaction of growth and development' takes place 'within the bond of affection formed between mother and child, and later, father and child', and if this attachment behaviour remains a feature of human behaviour throughout a person's life, then 'significant interaction, which is worthy of the name "human" always occurs in the context where affective feelings are present'.

Since 'the other', therefore, is much more than just a source of instinctual relief, it follows, in Dominian's opinion, that sexual activity loses both its vitality and its authenticity when it occurs without these affective feelings; that only in the presence of affectivity is full justice done to the meaning of sexuality; and that the separation of sex and affection is ultimately an illustration of dehumanization.

Love is an integral element in Dominian's vision of the human person at every stage in its development. He thinks that the attachment a child forms with its mother is a 'first experience of "falling in love"'; and that as we grow up we fall in love 'with several key people' culminating in a man or woman who becomes 'the exclusive object of our love'. Attachment behaviour is 'particularly pertinent' in this 'romantic' stage, since there are strong similarities between the attachment of an infant (AI) and that of a lover (LA).

Vision, sound and touch are important in both forms of attachment: 'we fall in love with people whose appearance and characteristics we like, whose voice we find pleasing, and with whom we feel comfortable in physical proximity.' Moreover 'both AI and

LA are reciprocal; when the mother or lover is not available, then the infant and lover become anxious, preoccupied, unable to concentrate. The infant and mother spend a good deal of time holding, touching, caressing, kissing, smiling, clinging to each other and so do lovers. There is a great deal of non-verbal communication between a mother and baby, and also primitive verbal sounds of cooing. Lovers also coo, talk baby language, and use non-verbal communication. This simple but highly effective communication is coupled with an intense awareness of the infant's inner world by the mother. Lovers show the same degree of mutual awareness of each other's inner world, called empathy.'

Bowlby's attachment theory is the foundation of Dominian's anthropology because Dominian believes that the capacity to form a bond is fundamental to loving at every stage in life. In *Sexual Integrity* he succinctly summarizes his stance. 'The human infant has the capacity to form one to one relationships through the mechanism of attachment. Human beings are built psychologically for personal attachments whose inner qualities are inclined towards exclusivity, reliability and predictability, reflecting the exclusive relationship of child and parent.'

The optimism of this vision of the human person is tempered in *Passionate and Compassionate Love* by Dominian's incorporation of recent work on Bowlby by Sternberg and Barnes in *The Psychology of Love*. Their research indicates that 'secure attachments' — those people who have successfully negotiated the childhood challenge of forming attachments — actually comprise only 50 per cent of the population; the other 50 per cent are equally divided into 'anxious attachments' and 'avoidant attachments'. Whereas the secure infant 'behaves and acts as if the mother is accessible to him even when she is out of sight', the anxious baby 'cries more than the secure baby, clings to her more and cannot use her as a safe base from which to explore the environment', while the avoidant baby 'tries to escape the gaze, contact and intimacy of mother'.

Childhood experiences, in Dominian's opinion, largely determine a person's capacity for intimacy; therefore it comes as no surprise to him that recent research has shown that these three types of attachment are found in adults as well as in infants. Secure attachments find it relatively easy to get close to people, feel comfortable depending on them, and are rarely worried about being abandoned. They are likely to consider themselves as popular and easy to get to know, and to view other people as generally well-intentioned. An anxious attachment is the outcome of a relationship between a child and parent in which the child did not 'receive an affirmative experience of being recognised, wanted and appreciated'; the wounded personality that developed is constantly worried as to how it will be received, and expects to be rejected. In an intimate relationship, an anxious attachment tends to live in constant dread of being abandoned, to see every other person as a threat to the relationship and to desire to be so close as almost to merge with its partner. Avoidant attachments, on the other hand, like to keep their distance, can appear undemonstrative, cold and aloof, find it difficult to trust, and be dependent, and feel uncomfortable in intimate relationships. 'It can be seen', Dominian concludes, 'that anxious and avoidant personalities have difficulties with their intimacy requirements, needing in turn too much or too little from their partners.'

The second neo-Freudian Dominian believes to have made a vital contribution to our understanding of the first year of life is D. W. Winnicott. Winnicott thought that in the first year of its life a baby developed a psyche which was to be distinguished from its mind; what a baby experienced physically became part of this psyche, which developed into an increasingly organized inner world in which somatic experiences were paramount. In addition Winnicott brought out clearly the intimate link between physical instinctual experiences and feeling good; in the first year of life the instinctual is largely based on food and elimination, but already, according to Winnicott, the infant is able to distinguish between what feels 'good' and what feels 'bad'.

As time elapses, a child gradually learns that it has to wait for food and postpone satisfaction. In Winnicott's opinion, this is the beginning of morality, based on inner control. He recognizes that the task of controlling the ruthless demands of internal instinct is not an easy one but he believes that the strictures of a loving mother can save the child from having to fight alone the battle for self-control. This control over instincts is 'something that the child learns more easily when boundaries are laid down by a loving parent' who, the child knows, loves and cares for it. Winnicott thinks that this natural evolution of self-control in the presence of a favourable parental environment 'brings about self-discipline without loss of spontaneity'.

Dominian believes that Winnicott's views have especial significance in guiding parents in the handling of such childish activities as little boys and girls playing with their genitals. In general, a child 'has to learn self-control' but yet 'retain a feeling that its impulses are good'. In this instance parents need to communicate a 'distinct feeling . . . that the genitalia are part of the whole body which is good', so that 'the child associates good feelings with the antecedents of its adult sexual life'.

The genius of Winnicott, according to Dominian, lies in the way he showed that the human psyche is the product of the earliest experiences of the physical in relation to the affectionate, and that the earliest physical dimension is instinctual. Essential to his thinking is the belief that the sense of love develops in a child from the very beginning of life, although the meaning of love in this first year alters as the child grows. It first means existing, breathing and being alive, then it means 'appetite, no awareness of the other person, but simply need and satisfaction'; and 'finally love means an integration on the part of the child of mother as a source of instinctual experience and of affectionate contact'. It follows that 'later taking and giving will be interrelated'.

Dominian learnt from Bowlby that the foundations of love are laid in the context of a bodily encounter at the beginning of life and drew the conclusion that only in the presence of affectivity can full justice be done to the meaning of sexual intercourse. He believes that Winnicott confirmed and complemented these insights by illustrating 'the essential human integration of instincts with the growing person, an integration which feels and is good, has its ultimate meaning in the context of a loving relationship and is open to control'; and by revealing that the connection between instinct and personal love was already visible in the first year of life and that 'instinct is part of the goodness of life which grows within the context of the loving parent–child relationship'.

The third neo-Freudian to influence Jack Dominian's anthropology is Eric Erikson. Dominian believes that there are two significant movements in personal relationships — 'first, one falls in love with another man or woman, then one proceeds to love that person' — and that this sequence is present from the first year of life. The forming of an attachment at that point can, in his opinion, be described as a 'falling in love', while the transition to 'loving' is made in the course of the child's development and during its interaction with parents, teachers and relatives. For an adult, this 'loving', or the maintenance of love, requires the acquisition and utilization of a number of skills and capacities: recognizing, accepting and respecting the beloved; understanding their need for autonomy and the taking of initiatives; maintaining trust and communication; resolving conflicts and forgiving; and preserving the balance between intimacy and separation. These particular capacities he believes to be the product of successfully negotiating the challenges of the different phases of childhood and adolescence as understood and presented by Erikson in his outline of human dynamic development.

The challenge of the first year of life, according to Erikson, is to establish a basic sense of trust, which is created by a mother combining a sensitive care of a baby's individual needs with a firm personal trustworthiness. This trust, in Dominian's opinion, is 'the criterion by which we feel safe in personal relationships'. It is essential for intimacy 'that we trust the people closest to us to be reliable. It is this reliability which gives us the basis of trust in the rest of our lives.'

Dominian then describes Erikson's view of the second and third year of life where he sees the major challenge as the acquisition of a sense of autonomy 'and how it relates to its opposites — shame and doubt'. Having established a relationship of trust the young child begins to separate from its mother and father. It learns to crawl, stand, walk, talk, dress and feed itself. Throughout, child and mother interact powerfully. The child learns by trial and error. Its primary efforts are either appreciated and praised, or treated in a derisory way and criticized. 'For Erikson, the autonomy stage becomes decisive for the ratio of love and hate, co-operation and wilfulness, freedom of self-expression and its suppression. From a lasting sense of self-control without loss of self-esteem comes a lasting sense of goodwill and pride: from a sense of loss of self-control and intrusive over-control comes a lasting propensity towards doubt and shame.'

In these years the child will cope by itself for increasingly longer periods before returning to its principal attachment figure. 'In psychological terms', according to Dominian, 'it is learning to internalise mother, that is to say, to keep her presence alive inside, in her physical absence.' He suggests that adult friendship or love requires a similar balance between closeness and separateness; and that a person's ability to internalize their spouse and avoid anxiety, fear or jealousy is largely dependent on the reliable presence of a parental figure in the early years of life. Jealousy, for example, he believes to be 'the fear of losing someone we love' which 'goes back to the child's fear of losing its key attachment figure'.

Growing autonomy leads to the first direct clash between mother and child. This, in Dominian's opinion, can be a momentous and devastating moment for a child, perhaps the first experience of being cut off from the love of its mother, and the first experience of external anger and aggression. Normally the conflict does not last long with mother forgiving, child feeling sorry and reconciliation taking place. But 'this cycle of anger, conflict, guilt, reparation and reconciliation endures throughout life and is an essential part of love' — between adults as well as between parent and child. Dominian thinks that if a person fails to negotiate this phase successfully in childhood, then in adult relationships he or she will find it difficult to apologize and to accept responsibility for their behaviour.

In the fourth and fifth year of life, Erikson believes a child needs to acquire a sense of initiative. In addition, he or she becomes much more conscious of the feeling of being recognized, wanted and appreciated, and has a clearer idea of the difference between acceptance and rejection. Dominian points out how important the consequent self-esteem is for later relationships. 'If we feel lovable, then we allow people to get close, and to love us. We are not afraid of what they will discover when they approach us. We have nothing to hide.' In contrast 'those who are unsure of themselves seek to boost their self-esteem by additional embellishment'.

Towards the end of this phase a child enters a new world, that of school. The challenge there is to acquire what Erikson describes as the 'industry' skills. So far, self-esteem, that feeling of being lovable, has grown through parental nurturing and has been dependent upon the child's ability to experience those feelings of being recognized, wanted and appreciated. Now, however, cognitive training begins in earnest. During the school years the child learns to earn recognition by producing things, and self-esteem is considerably influenced by the results of and reaction to its industry and achievement: 'school with its marks, reports and examination results, offers a visible indication of success and failure.' Dominian believes that this dual basis of self-esteem, derived from home and school respectively, is potentially conflictual and can have important implications for adult love. If a child has not acquired 'the feeling of unconditional love on the basis of being a person in his or her own right, worthy of love', then love and approval will be experienced as 'solely dependent on achievement'. If that happens, the child, when it becomes an adult, might well have little expectation of being loved for his or her own worth and act as if 'every

bit of approval has to be earned through performance'. Dominian
thinks that husbands and wives brought up in this way only expect
appreciation when they fulfil their roles at home and work, and can
be extremely critical of themselves and their partner if they fail to
deliver what they perceive to be the appropriate and required
behaviour.

School life also introduces a child to another facet of love — what
Dominian calls 'the concept of social justice'. A child enters the world
of many children in the community of the school and has to learn to
live in a more impersonal environment where rules and regulations
govern behaviour. Between the ages of seven and ten children reach
a point of development when they no longer accept the authority
of their parents and teachers unconditionally and feel treated
unfairly when parents and teachers use their authority without adequate reason. Dominian believes that 'the feeling of being asked
to do something which does not respect one's integrity . . . forms
a deep groove in an emerging personality' and consequently that
an adult's sense of justice is greatly influenced by their childhood
experience of the way rules and regulations were enforced.

The prelude to Erikson's next phase, adolescence, is puberty,
occurring somewhere between the ages of ten and fourteen. During
puberty the physical development of secondary sexual characteristics is complemented by marked psychological changes. 'The
adolescent distances himself or herself from the parents, particularly
the parent of the opposite sex. This sexual withdrawal is accompanied by heterosexual attraction and the increasing interest of the
two sexes in each other develops.'

Erikson believes that adolescence, lasting from the age of twelve to
the early twenties, is a time of role confusion, since adolescents are
on the top step of childhood and the bottom one of adulthood. The
challenge of this phase, therefore, is the attainment of a personal
identity. Dominian thinks this happens through a growing independence from one's parents, the search for a suitable alternative to them
and eventually the forming of a new attachment. In the area of
sexuality, in particular, this phase is a time of discovery. Each individual now has the potential for genital activity and the desire to seek
sexual relationships but first needs to 'become acquainted with
his/her sexuality' and to 'learn how to be a sexual person'.

Dominian recognizes that one of the most common ways for
adolescents to discover their sexuality is through masturbation. He
acknowledges that in the Roman Catholic tradition masturbation has

been viewed as sinful but he disagrees with this tradition because he believes it to be a legitimate way in this particular phase to become familiar with oneself as a sexual person. However, the same does not hold true for sexual intercourse. 'The fact that sexual intercourse is possible does not mean that it is meaningful in the context of this phase of life' while 'neither human development nor sexual morality envisages relationships at this time' within which it should take place.

The arguments that Dominian presents for the unsuitability of sexual intercourse for adolescents illustrate his overall understanding of the human person and of human sexuality. The foundation of his approach is his belief that from the very beginning of life a person's instincts are not separate entities but are integrated in the whole personality, shaped and controlled in an interaction with parents who relate in love; and indeed that it is impossible and inauthentic at any stage of life to separate instincts from feelings and the rest of the personality.

In addition, Dominian thinks that physical sexual instincts are but one element within the whole sexual dimension of the personality and that this personality is designed for forming adult attachments. Childhood and adolescence present successive developmental challenges, the successful negotiation of which brings abilities which enable an individual to engage in loving personal relationships and which are essential for the maintenance of love between two adults. Adolescence itself, therefore, he sees as a time for sexual attachment in the broadest sense, one in which young people should test each other for mutual suitability through companionship: 'it takes a long time and a number of friendships to discover a partner who is capable of establishing a lifelong relationship which is exclusive, permanent and faithful — the characteristics of marriage in most societies.'

Sexual intercourse in general is not designed for the discernment of personal suitability: 'sexual intercourse does not help to discover whether a potential partner is trustworthy, reliable, has or has not a quick temper, is capable of loving or being loved, is caring, affectionate, a reliable worker, honest, considerate, faithful, capable of emotional closeness, sensitive but not over-sensitive, stable but can take initiative, disciplined but can enjoy life, conscientious but not rigid, flexible but not indecisive.' Rather, sexual intercourse, once an attachment has been formed, has a 'unique capacity for affirming personal choice and sealing a relationship — for maintaining rather than creating bonds'.

It follows that Dominian does not believe that it is necessary to test sexual compatibility before marriage. In his opinion, sexual affinity and fulfilment follow closely on from personal amiability; 'the key to satisfactory sex is satisfactory relationship.' Nor is it impossible to abstain from sex until then: 'for myself and millions of my own generation who observed the rule of premarital chastity, the idea that instincts are so overwhelming that they cannot be contained is novel.'

These views, however, do not mean that Dominian considers sexual intercourse to be unimportant. Rather he sees it as 'a particularly rich and significant experience whose full meaning can only be realised in the context of a permanent, committed and faithful relationship, signifying the full donation of one person to another in a relationship of love'. Nor does he underplay its specifically physical dimension. In *Sexual Integrity* he states that from the time of puberty, sexual arousal and attraction are designed for the sexual act; while in *Passionate and Compassionate Love* he gives a detailed analysis of the different ways in which men and women are aroused and how this affects preparations for making love. He acknowledges that from a physiological perspective 'the whole point of sexual intercourse is to experience and give erotic pleasure' and therefore that 'the object of the exercise is for the couple to reach mutual orgasm with its exquisite pleasure and joy'. However Dominian is characteristically keen to stress the need to integrate the physical with the psychological, an integration once more with its roots in infancy and childhood: 'The adult sexual act appears on the surface to have no connection with that era, but this is not the case. In the process of genital interaction, the two bodies make an intimate, secure, close rhythmic contact which has a strong reminder of the intimate closeness between baby and mother with the same rhythm of intimacy.'

In *Sexual Integrity* Dominian examines the different elements present in sexual intercourse and proposes a hierarchy of values. First, it is an 'act marked by pronounced sexual and physical excitation which, when consummated in an orgasm, gives intense pleasure and relief of the accompanying tension'. Secondly, 'when penis–vagina penetration occurs, the depositing of semen in the vagina, and hence procreation, becomes a possibility'. Finally, 'there is a possibility of a personal encounter between a man and woman possessing the dimension of love. Genital unity becomes the symbol of personal donation in which two people feel they receive each other wholly and in a committed manner.'

For Dominian the supreme value is this dimension of personal love — the 'indispensable quality', since its presence makes it possible for the partners to deepen their significance and attachment for each other each time they make love. The second most important value is the procreative ability inherent in the act; on this potential he believes the world depends for its continuity. The third value is the realization of pleasure, which he sees as intrinsic to the act and an essential part of its goodness since it aids human attraction and bonding. He stresses that this dimension is to be cherished and celebrated but he also thinks that human integrity is disturbed if it is sought as an end in itself.

Dominian believes that the meaning and morality of each act of sexual intercourse depends on the circumstances in which it takes place and that the major distinction that should be made is between casual sex and sex that occurs between couples living in exclusive and committed relationships. In his opinion sexual intercourse in an exclusive and committed relationship has much greater authenticity and integrity than casual sex since it nurtures the personal dimensions of love, thus preserving what he perceives as the most important of the values at stake.

The ideal place for the expression of such intimacy is marriage. He presents three main reasons. First, he recognizes the reality of human frailty and thinks that the deeper the commitment the greater the protection against this frailty. 'Just as there is a spectrum of human sexuality between the casual and the committed' so 'there is a range of human commitment ranging from promise to vows. A promise is not a vow, which realises the deepest elements of human truth.'

Secondly, he is convinced that relationships are more than just a personal encounter and that in every person and in every relationship there is an essential social dimension. He believes that the decision to relate permanently to another human being in love and to raise a family is as much a social as a personal statement and requires the involvement and support of society. Therefore he thinks that a wedding ceremony is necessary to ratify the social assent to the personal commitment of the couple and to act as a guarantee to their personal love.

Finally, Dominian addresses the issue of human integrity, which he understands as the realization of human potential. He believes that for two people to make love with integrity all the potential latent in the act has to be fulfilled. The three main 'values' of sexual

ERRATUM

The publishers regret that the wrong text has been printed on p. 111. The correct text for this page is as follows:

Jack Dominian's knowledge of the causes and consequences of marital breakdown has convinced him of the need for a comprehensive programme for the support of marriage. A key element in the programme he himself puts forward is the repeated presentation and communication of a positive vision of marriage as the best way for human beings to fulfil their potential. In a good marriage Dominian believes that a couple, building on the foundation that the continuity, reliability and predictability of a permanent relationship gives them, and channelling the energy that comes from sexual intercourse, can sustain each other, heal each other and encourage each other to grow.

One of the distinctive features of Dominian's overall approach is his attraction to 'lists'. Thus he suggests that there are five dimensions in the marital relationship and three phases in its lifecycle; five characteristics of sexual intercourse in a committed relationship; three components in the framework of marital permanence; and, perhaps the most frequently repeated of all these delineations, three characteristics of marital love: sustaining, healing and growth.

The first of these three components is sustaining love. As Dominian writes in *Make or Break*, 'the essential feature of marriage is the presence of a relationship between a man and a woman. This relationship is first and foremost a sustaining experience. This sustaining is social, emotional, sexual, intellectual and spiritual.' Couples have always sustained each other on the economic and social level — setting up a home, running it on the basis of complementary responsibility, providing company for each other, doing things together, participating in the wider communities of their family, friends and neighbourhood, and looking after each other's material

intercourse — the deepening of personal love, the potential for procreation and the realization of pleasure — can, in his opinion, never
be isolated from the sexual instinct which has been integrated within
the whole personality from infancy onwards. In consequence, if any
act of sexual intercourse is to realize the richness of its potential,
it requires the secure framework of love that only marriage can
offer — the framework of exclusiveness, faithfulness and permanency, which 'all human beings long for and have been conditioned
to in childhood'.

Jack Dominian's solid psychological training ensures that his
anthropology, although eclectic, is coherent and soundly rooted,
even if he acknowledges that his overall methodology — 'I'm a very
intuitive person, I feel the truth in my bones' — is 'a very unscien-
tific way of operating'. However, he does not have the same professional background in philosophy and theology. Indeed he recognizes
his own strong bias against philosophy — 'existential philosophers
make some sense to me. The others leave me cold' — and seems,
too, to take a certain pride in denying that he has been influenced by any particular theologians. He has read Rahner and
Schillebeeckx, but 'they confirmed my position' rather than ini-
tiated it.

Dominian's starting-point is always inductive and intuitive.
He takes his own experience and his vision of the human person,
synthesises them with his understanding of the Gospels, and lets
them then dictate his 'theology' and his attitude to official Church
pronouncements. Those two seminal articles written in 1966 —
'Sexuality and psychology' and 'Vatican II and marriage' — both
vividly illustrate this 'method', which gains in conviction what it
lacks in logic or intellectual rigour. He has never in any of his books
specifically presented his theological assumptions and beliefs but as
with his anthropology it is possible to extract a coherent synthesis
from *Sexual Integrity* and *Passionate and Compassionate Love*.

Jack Dominian believes that 'this vast mystery we call the world
is not a chance happening but the fruit of a living and loving God
who created it out of love, and made love the supreme characteristic
to be lived in this world and to be shared with the Creator in the
next, so that wherever authentic love exists, God is present'.

This God who creates the world is a God who never ceases to
dialogue with his people. 'This dialogue was brought to perfection
in the incarnation when God took on the fulness of being human.
Jesus showed us that love and compassion are the principal means

of responding to our neighbour; at the same time he raised human integrity to an unprecedented level of perfection.'

Dominian thinks that the scriptural origins of this love of neighbour are to be found in the law of Moses. He cites the book of Leviticus: 'You will not exact vengeance on or bear any sort of grudge against, the members of your race, but will love your neighbour as yourself. I am Yahweh' (Leviticus 19:18). Jesus, in his opinion, 'picks up where Leviticus leaves off'. He quotes from St Luke's Gospel:

> And now a lawyer stood up, and to test him, asked 'Master, what must I do to inherit eternal life?' He said to him, 'What is written in the Law? What is your reading of it?' He replied, 'You must love the Lord your God with all your heart, with all your soul, and with all your strength, and with all your mind, and your neighbour as yourself.' Jesus said to him, 'You have answered right, do this and life is yours.' (Luke 10:25–28)

When the lawyer then asks Jesus 'Who is my neighbour?' he receives 'the majestic reply that has reverberated through the centuries, namely the story of the Good Samaritan'. The Jews, according to Dominian, were aware of the commandment to love their neighbour but interpreted that neighbour as a fellow Jew: 'what Jesus did was to enlarge the concept of neighbour to everyone.'

However, 'it is in the Johannine gospel and epistles, and the Pauline epistles', rather than the synoptic gospels, that 'we have the most powerful pronouncements of love'. Dominian thinks that an analysis of Paul's great oration to the Corinthians clarifies 'the essential components of personal love', while John 'gives us the ultimate significance of love' when he writes: 'My dear friends, let us love each other since love is from God and everyone who loves is a child of God and knows God. Whoever fails to love does not know God, because God is love' (1 John 4:7–8).

'The summation of all Christian teaching', in Dominian's opinion, is this call to love our neighbour and this revelation that God is love. God is the unseen and unknown force that holds the world — and each individual — together. 'He does that in and through love. As long as we are loving, then we are in his presence and he is in us.' Indeed 'personal love is the ultimate criterion by which all human behaviour has to be assessed'.

Dominian thinks that the Church is primarily a sign of the revelation that God has 'lived, died and overcome death'; Christians, therefore, are 'a community of believers who give testimony to this truth'. The Church's task is to be 'a sacrament of Christ'; 'each successive generation has to exercise love and compassion and realise a little bit more of the Kingdom of God.'

Dominian accepts that 'in its wisdom, the Church makes rules and regulations about human behaviour' in order to 'encourage people to perfect themselves, and to reflect the image of God in them'. But it is love rather than these regulations that is 'at the centre of being Christian' as 'the ultimate criteria of our faith is belief in and worship of the Trinity in and through love'. Furthermore, 'the rules of morality which assist us in this goal' are liable to change: Dominian believes that God is still speaking to the world 'as he has always done' and that the task of theology, therefore, is to reflect on this continuing dialogue in such a way that 'knowledge of the truth unfolds' and Christians are enabled to reflect the personality of Christ.

Dominian's main concern and interest, in theology as in life, lies in the domain of sexuality and marriage. He implicitly acknowledges this orientation in both *Sexual Integrity* and *Passionate and Compassionate Love*. In *Sexual Integrity*, he asserts that 'human sexuality combines attraction, pairing, the maintenance of the bond and procreation. Between them they form the foundation of family life and society. In many respects, this energy is the cornerstone of our humanity, and as such deserves a central place in Christian life.' He wants to give it this place by showing that 'human beings and their sexuality reflect and point to the divine nature' and therefore that 'sexuality has been made sacred'. Similarly, in the opening chapter of *Passionate and Compassionate Love* he writes that 'one of the purposes of this book is to show that marital love constitutes for most human beings their central experience of God, and their most precious neighbour is first their spouse, then their children, and finally the neighbour who is near or far away'.

Dominian's 'theology' of sexuality and marriage is built on three key texts in Genesis. The first is Genesis 1:27: 'God created man in the image of himself; in the image of God he created him; male and female he created them.' For Dominian this reveals that 'sexuality with all its richness is of the very essence of the godhead'; that 'God is shown to be a mystery which contains a sexual dimension of the constituents of maleness and femaleness'; and that men and women thus 'reflect a basic characteristic of the divine'.

The second text is Genesis 2:18–25, the second creation account:

Yahweh God said 'It is not right that the man should be alone. I shall make him a helper.' Then Yahweh God made the man fall into a deep sleep. And, while he was asleep, he took one of his ribs and closed the flesh up again forthwith. Yahweh God fashioned the rib he had taken from the man into a woman, and brought her to the man. And the man said, 'This one at last is bone of my bones and flesh of my flesh. She is to be called woman, because she was taken from man.' That is why a man leaves his father and mother and becomes attached to his wife, and they become one flesh.

This basic orientation of the couple towards each other is, in Dominian's opinion, 'the central pillar of God's plan for humanity' and means that 'the key to understanding human sexuality is to be found in the concept of relationship'. The 'ultimate consummation' of this relationship is 'the oneness' of sexual intercourse, which reflects the mystery of the Trinity 'where the three persons are constantly in a relationship of love, which makes them one, and yet they retain their separate identity, just as the couple do'. Moreover 'the priority' is clearly the relationship first and procreation second — 'it is only when the couple form a relationship that revelation shows should be permanent, that procreation is possible.'

The third passage cited by Dominian from Genesis is 1:28-31:

God blessed them, saying to them 'Be fruitful, multiply, fill the earth and subdue it. Be masters of the fish of the sea, the birds of the heaven, and all the living creatures that move on earth' . . . God saw all he had made, and indeed it was very good.

Dominian thinks that 'the key words here are that the creation of men and women with the distinct blessing of fruitfulness was very good'. God created the world and then 'delegated its continuation to mankind' so that human beings, 'as viceroys, have the task of continuing the human race through the gift of sexuality'. This sexuality is 'a precious gift which in fact determines the whole structure of human relations'; the man–woman encounter is 'the fundamental unit of sexuality on which the world was built'.

In *Passionate and Compassionate Love* Dominian makes explicit what he believes is implicit in these three passages; 'in God's plan for mankind, there is a union between a man and a woman, who are of equal worth, which provides the fundamental relationship for the sexes, within which new life can start. Although procreation is clearly a basic construct of the unity of the sexes, it is their relationship with each other that provides the fundamental background.'

Dominian also cites other passages in the Old Testament; he thinks that the 'basic goodness' of sexuality is underlined in that 'apotheosis of erotic love situated in a biblical setting', the Song of Songs. He also asserts that when the prophets Hosea, Jeremiah, Ezekiel and Isaiah use marriage as a symbol of the intimacy between God and Israel, they reveal that love is the true heart of marriage and that love within marriage 'becomes a reflection of the divine mystery of God's love'.

The New Testament, outside of the Pauline and Johannine epistles, does not seem to greatly influence Dominian's basic theological vision. The fact Jesus performed his first miracle at the wedding feast of Cana in his opinion indicates Jesus 'must have approved of marriage if he associated it with such an intervention'. He notes the way Jesus directed attention to a person's inner desires — 'if a man looks at a woman lustfully . . .' (Matthew 5:27) — and his demand for a much higher standard of chastity than before. Dominian cites Jesus' distinctive attitude to women as heralding 'the advent of the equality of the worth of the sexes'; and he speculates as to why Jesus remained unmarried, suggesting that the exclusivity required by marriage was not compatible with his mission and that, anyway, Jesus as Son of God 'belonged to the divine world of relationship in which the Trinity had its own special inner world where marriage did not feature'.

However, Dominian does acknowledge that the combination of Jesus' virgin birth and single state have 'left Christianity a problem how to present marriage' (and, by implication, sexuality); and that this is only partially offset by Paul in his letter to the Ephesians (Ephesians 5:25, 28–32) adopting the same symbol of marriage for the relationship of love between Christ and his Church that the prophets had used for the relationship between God and Israel.

Nonetheless, Dominian feels able to assert that his 'perusal of the Old and New Testaments testifies to the centrality of sexuality and marriage' in the Scriptures. He finds present in them a consistent line of thought that understands 'human sexuality as something fundamentally good, a secular reality ordained for the attraction of the sexes, expressing love in the unity of the couple in marriage and being fruitful in children'. Furthermore, the body 'which Christ took on in the incarnation' is 'the instrument through which the race is continued, and in the process, puts into practice, each successive generation, the fruits of love'. It follows that God 'has given us this world to explore, and each other to love' and that 'the central way we do this is in an intimate relationship of personal love'. Such a relationship 'reflects the divine mystery of God himself, the mystery being shown in person, relationship and love', which ultimately finds expression in 'the divine dynamism of three persons, constantly relating in love with each other in the Trinity'.

The richness of the vision of sexuality which Dominian discovers in the Scriptures is not 'continued in the Christian tradition'. He asserts that sex there is surrounded 'at worst by suspicion and hostility' while, at best, 'its integrity is preserved in marriage primarily when it serves as a procreative function'. Indeed he believes that 'it is no exaggeration to say that for most of the 2000 years of Christianity, the voice of the Church welcomed sexuality principally as a channel for new life', while 'its inner world of rich meaning and the link with love were occasionally hinted at but never taken up in substance'.

This leaves Dominian with a dilemma. 'How is it then that the Holy Spirit, while protecting the Church from seeing sex and procreation as evil — which was the view of early heresies like Gnosticism — nevertheless failed to promote its unique meaning within the Church?' Rather than answering this question directly, he analyses the reasons for such a limited view: the need felt in the early years of Christianity to emphasize virginity because of the virgin birth, the desire to pay 'the right attention to Our Lady' and the fact that Jesus 'was a celibate and Paul had a predilection for that state'; the influence of Greek thought with its stress on detachment from passion — 'Epicurus is said to have declared "Nobody was ever the better for the carnal act and a man may be thankful if he was not definitely the worse" '; the insidious effect of the Manichaean heresy with its hostility to sexuality; a similar hostility visible in certain Greek and Latin Fathers of the Church, especially St Augustine 'who had such marked personal problems in sexual matters'; and in those early centuries, and thereafter, the lack of status accorded to women which ensured that 'no connection' was made between sex, procreation and human love and therefore that the Church's procreative-orientated approach possessed 'a ring of truth'.

However, although he recognizes the importance of these factors, Dominian thinks that the most important single reason for the poverty of the Christian understanding of sexuality through the centuries has lain in the predominance of a celibate clergy and the consequent neglect of the laity and of 'their sacrament', the sacrament of marriage. He believes 'a rich theology of sex and marriage needs the married to contribute' and yet 'for hundreds of years, the laity have hardly existed in their own right'. Indeed in the Catholic Church, the laity and married 'assumed theological significance only after the Second Vatican Council and have yet to find their voice and indeed the confidence to articulate their thoughts'.

Dominian does acknowledge that the Protestant tradition with its married clergy has also, in his opinion, 'failed to make a distinctive contribution to the theology of sexuality' and that 'in fairness to the whole Christian tradition, it must be said that, given the social and psychological limitations of understanding that have prevailed for the major part of the Church's history, the lack of theological progress in sexual matters is not surprising'. However, that merely serves to confirm his belief that 'in this area of human thought and experience, Christian tradition is important yet limited'. He is 'at one with the mind of the Church in wishing to emphasize the importance of tradition in assessing moral matters' but he is also convinced that these limitations ensure the need for 'radical alterations to moral principles'.

Such alterations do not present Dominian with theological difficulties since he believes that 'God continuously reveals the richness of his creation as human beings unfold and realise its truths through the means he places in their hands', among the most important of which are 'contemporary psychological insights'. These alterations to moral principles are morally authentic when 'the results which emerge are consistent with revealed truths in the scriptures'.

One significant example of such authenticity, for Dominian, is the relatively recent 'realisation' that when a couple make love, it is the loving components of the act rather than 'the biology of coitus' which is of primary significance. Such a shift in outlook is acceptable to him since he believes it is 'congruent with revelation'.

In *Sexual Integrity* Dominian analyses the concept of 'natural law' — which he understands to be, with Scripture, the main source for Catholic teaching on sexuality. He asserts that 'in its natural law theology the Church has considered it possible to reach moral conclusions through which all men and women can see the truth about human behaviour independently of revelation' by reflecting upon the reality of God's human creation. He proceeds to examine what he thinks are the origins of that teaching — the belief of St Augustine that God's eternal law was 'impressed' on his creatures, and of St Thomas Aquinas that by examining this eternal law in the nature of things, human beings 'could reach God's intentions of how they should be used and not abused'.

Dominian claims that Aquinas discovered three fundamental dynamisms with moral implications: 'the first and most basic is the one we share with all created creatures, preservation': hence all activity that involves killing — like euthanasia — is wrong. The second principle, again shared with all creatures, is the drive to ensure the survival of the species, which Dominian calls 'the biology of procreation'. From this principle 'all sexual behaviour could be organised'; indeed, 'a great deal of traditional Roman Catholic sexual ethics depends on this concept'. The third principle 'applies to human beings alone and is a natural inclination with two characteristics: our rationality, leading to the pursuit of truth; and life in community, with all the resulting moral implications of love'.

Dominian states that 'no one can underestimate the value of natural law and the invaluable contributions that this concept, heavily influenced by the thought of Aquinas, has made to Catholic thought, to all Christianity, and to society'. However, he also asserts that the extensive advantages the concept of natural law had in the past have recently been offset by the multiplication of views about what constitutes human nature 'leading to many difficulties and problems'; and he suggests that the recognition that there were difficulties was responsible for a 'shift of emphasis from nature to person' in the Second Vatican Council. The Council 'did not abrogate moral principles drawn from natural law'; rather it emphasized 'not human nature as such but the human person' as the fundamental source of morality. 'The dignity of the human person' was 'central', for example, to 'the immensely important section on "Marriage and the family in the modern world" ' in *Gaudium et Spes* — and, indeed, to the whole of that document.

Dominian thinks that this shift 'has accelerated a process of renewal in moral theology, based on natural law' which had started before the Council began. 'At least two schools of thought have emerged' since then; one, the more traditional, he associates with an American theologian, Germain Grisez; the other, 'consequentialism', he views as more likely to take up new positions. Dominian's sympathies are visibly with the latter school.

Such a fluid and unsettled theological situation leads to controversy and disagreement about the moral status of certain actions. Dominian believes that the soundest moral formulations are those in which 'scripture, tradition and natural law are clearly and irrevocably in agreement'. He thinks that some issues like fornication and adultery are clear-cut but that others, like the moral status of divorce and contraception, are more difficult to judge; regarding the former, 'there are arguments about the scriptural sayings on divorce' while 'in the absence of scriptural teaching, the position on contraception has been very problematical'.

How should a Catholic make his or her decision when there are conflicting views on the moral value of a particular action? Before answering this question Dominian examines the nature of the teaching authority of the Church, the Magisterium, and its relationship to the individual conscience. The New Testament, in his opinion, 'recognises two moral authorities': 'firstly, there is the Johannine view' that the believer receives an anointing of the Spirit 'which makes it unnecessary for anyone to instruct the one anointed, as the Spirit teaches everything, and it is the truth'; this approach 'is connected with the concept of conscience'. Secondly 'the view is present in the New Testament, particularly in Matthew's Gospel', that some members of the community have a teaching role which gives them authority to offer moral guidance to their fellow Christians. Dominian claims that 'this dual recognition of external teaching and an internal enlightenment, which influences final choice, remains the orthodox teaching in the Roman Catholic Church to this very day'.

He then takes a historical perspective. He believes that 'gradually, and in particular during the last hundred years, the Magisterium has been concentrated in the hands of bishops, and, in particular, the Pope centred at Rome'. As a result the Church came to divide itself into a 'teaching' Church made up of the hierarchy and particularly the Papacy, and a 'learning' Church, containing everybody else. This tendency culminated in the First Vatican Council with its definition of Papal infallibility. However, 'the Second Vatican Council was aware of this excessive concentration of power in the hands of the Pope and was concerned to situate papal authority in the wider context of all the bishops'.

Dominian cites a passage in *Lumen Gentium* as an example of the way the Council re-emphasized the importance of the local bishop: 'in matters of faith and morals, the bishops speak in the name of Christ, and the faithful are to accept their teaching and adhere to it with a religious assent of soul.' However, he asserts that 'in the course of the history of the Church, more and more power was appropriated by the priest and the bishop and, in particular, the Pope' with the result that 'the laity were left with little but to be taught and to obey'. That 'cannot be right' and so 'the Second Vatican Council began the necessary correction'.

Dominian thinks that the enormous tensions that have unfolded in the Church since the Council have partly been caused by the Council's vision of 'the Church as a whole participating in the priestly, kingly and prophetic characteristics of Christ' and by the subsequent attempts to restore 'a balance between clergy and laity, hierarchy and Rome'. He is particularly interested in 'the question of prophecy' which he understands as examining 'through whom does the Holy Spirit speak in the life of the Church?' He believes that the Council made it clear that the teaching authority of the bishops is prophetic, but that it also revealed that the laity, too, share in the overall prophetic activity of the Church. He quotes *Gaudium et Spes*: 'Christ the Great Prophet . . . continually fulfils his prophetic office . . . not only through the hierarchy . . . but also through the laity.' From this he draws the controversial conclusion that 'it is thus inconceivable, after the Second Vatican Council, to think that truth in the Church is only to be found in official teaching'.

Dominian fully accepts that 'someone has to teach and that that someone is the bishop, in particular the bishop of Rome' but he is also convinced that what is taught 'must have the marks of discernment'; it must 'appeal to people's minds and feelings, that is, have the ring of intellectual truth, and at the same time feel right'. Otherwise 'human beings cannot give their assent'. However that will only happen if the laity are consulted and enabled 'to make their own contribution'.

Dominian quotes three passages from *Gaudium et Spes* which he believes indicates the Council's support for such an approach. The first recognizes that the Church does not have all the answers; it 'requires special help' and needs to 'rely on those who live in the world, are versed in different institutions and specialities and grasp their innermost significance'. Indeed it is 'the task of the entire People of God . . . to hear, distinguish and interpret the many voices of our age, and to judge them in the light of the divine Word'. The second passage declares that when difficulties arise in family life 'the Christian instincts of the faithful, the upright moral consciences of men, and the wisdom and experience of persons versed in social sciences will have much to contribute'. The third suggests that 'in pastoral care, appropriate use must be made not only of theological principles, but also of the findings of the secular sciences, especially of psychology and of sociology. Thus the faithful can be brought to live the faith in a more thorough and mature way.'

In addition, Dominian believes that the Council accepts the concept of loyal dissent. He cites *Gaudium et Spes* as stating that 'an individual layman, by reasons of the knowledge, competence or outstanding ability he may enjoy, is permitted and sometimes even obliged to express his opinion in things which concern the good of the Church'; when such occasions arise, this must 'be done in truth, in courage, and in prudence, with reverence and charity towards those who by reason of their sacred office represent the person of Christ'.

Thus every Catholic, in Dominian's opinion, 'must ultimately obey his conscience, the final arbiter in moral choices', although before doing so he or she 'should be familiar with the teaching and give serious attention to the case made by the Church'. He himself finds that he dissents 'from a number of positions in sexual ethics'. He believes that 'in the deliberations of moral theology, the laity have a vital and necessary contribution' and that moral theology has no validity without their input; but that they have not been allowed to make this contribution to Church teaching on sexual matters. As a result, in this area the Church's 'teaching is flawed to a large extent', and its authority, and 'ultimately the presence of Christ in the world', is undermined. The tension Dominian experiences is 'a personal agony' and 'a source of deep pain' but he feels bound to obey his conscience. Therefore, when he writes or speaks 'I try to give an accurate formulation of the teaching of the Church, put forward the arguments on its behalf, and then, where I dissent, put forward the other side, and let people make up their mind'.

For all these attempts to defend his approach theologically, Dominian's anthropology is governed by his psychology rather than his theology. Nowhere is this more visible than in his presentation of the principle of sexual integrity as 'the predominant basis for sexual ethics in the twenty-first century'. Sexual integrity is a term he prefers to chastity, because 'it is a concept that applies to everyone, believers and non-believers', since 'everyone has a responsibility to apply their sexuality in a way that does justice to their humanity'; and because chastity, in his opinion, is 'associated with a hostile restriction on sexual pleasure'.

Sexual integrity is based on the assumption that 'human beings are programmed in childhood to love, and, after puberty, towards sexual attraction, which leads to pairing, and the formation of a bond, called marriage, within which love is expressed'. Sexual attraction is 'the single most important force in human beings' intended, first 'to form and maintain bonds', and secondly 'to continue the race'. It follows that 'the main purpose of human sexuality is no longer biological but personal in which love is the predominant theme'.

Within that framework, Dominian understands sexual integrity as revolving round the concepts of person, relationship and love. It is 'concerned with following the development of persons in relationships, which acquire and express love'. It is present at conception when an act of love sets a new life in motion, and is concerned initially with the relationship between parents and children through which the essentials of human love are learned. The first responsibility of parents is to help their children learn what it means to be truly loved, a task that is 'mainly social and psychological'. After puberty, the emphasis is on the interaction of the sexes, mutual exploration and the establishment of pairing. During this phase sexual intercourse is not compatible with sexual integrity since 'it is not primarily an act which defines suitability for partnership'.

Once 'bonding has been established', sexual integrity is concerned with taking 'every social, physical and psychological care that the physical act becomes an intact channel for this bonding through the expression of love'. In addition, it seeks to avoid anything that disrupts the bond, such as adultery and marital breakdown. Dominian considers this not only to be 'consistent with human evolution' but also to make sense of 'the traditional Judaeo-Christian warnings against fornication, adultery and divorce, which form a triad whose avoidance preserves the family, the basic unit of society all over the world'.

Dominian believes that this concept of sexual integrity offers Christianity a chance at last to respond to the challenge which, in his opinion, has been facing it for a considerable time — the provision of a new basis for sexual morality. 'For over 3,000 years, the Judaeo-Christian tradition has based its sexual morality on the link between intercourse and procreation.' The advent of contraception has severed this link and ushered in a new era 'in which there is a pronounced shift in sexuality from biology to personal love'. However, the Catholic Church has refused to accept this break between sexual intercourse and procreation. This he thinks has been a major factor in the churches' failure in credibility in the area of sexuality.

Dominian acknowledges that contraception has made sexual integrity much harder 'because it has reinforced a human frailty to participate in coitus in a variety of conditions in which bonding is not central', and that within the context of bonding 'we have a long way to go to find efficient and satisfactory contraceptives'. However, in general, he views contraception in a positive light as 'a distinct extension of God's gift to man to subdue creation and reveal more clearly' the basic design and purpose of sexual inter-course — the assistance of bonding' — rather than procreation.

Dominian considers that in the present age 'the whole ethos of contemporary human relationship is a realization of human inte-grity' and 'men and women are seeking integrity in the presence of each other'. However, society has tended to concentrate on the erotic at the expense of the personal and 'has to realise that unfet-tered sexual instincts do not represent authentic human behaviour'. Christianity, on the other hand, has never had difficulty in under-standing the importance of personal love, but has failed to rejoice sufficiently in the erotic. He thinks that the principle of sexual integrity will enable Christianity finally to present an authoritative basis for modern sexual morality, and in so doing, will help society to realize that the fulness of sexuality is found in the conjunction of the personal and the erotic.

If anthropology is the basis of Dominian's presentation of sexual integrity, his free-flowing theology gives it a concluding flourish. Dominian believes that the principle of sexual integrity can even shed light on the mystery of sexuality within God himself: 'God in whose image we have been created, does not use sexuality for the purpose of procreation'; however, 'sexuality is the basic force of love which sustains an everlasting relationship of dynamic unity between the three Persons of the Trinity, while respecting their unique individuality in the same way that coitus achieves it for the human couple'.

CHAPTER FIVE

The changing nature of marriage and the marital lifecycle

Jack Dominian's experience as a marriage counsellor in the late 1950s and early 1960s caused 'the first and deepest crisis' in his life. It transformed his attitude to the Church and Church authority; it caused him to rethink his whole understanding of marriage and marital breakdown; and because he came to believe that divorce was the most important social evil in Western society, responsible for untold acute personal agonies and much else, it enormously influenced the subsequent direction of his life and work.

Dominian's greatest area of interest and expertise in the last thirty years has been in his analysis of the causes and consequences of marital breakdown. To that end he has devoted endless hours counselling marriages in difficulties; he has established and developed a Marriage Research Centre, creating a strategy to combat marital breakdown based on the concept 'research into practice for prevention'; and he has written an enormous number of articles and four books commissioned by four different publishers: *Marital Breakdown* (Penguin, 1968); *Marital Pathology* (Darton, Longman & Todd, 1980); *Make or Break: An Introduction to Marriage Counselling* (SPCK, 1984); and *An Introduction to Marital Problems* (Fount, 1986).

Dominian's psychiatric training has meant that for most of the last thirty years he has sought to explain marital breakdown on psychological grounds. While respecting the view of some of his colleagues that 'nature' — the biological in a broad sense — is the dominant contributor to the adult personality, as a dynamically-orientated psychiatrist, he has always emphasized 'nurture' — the experience of the child in the family environment. He has repeatedly stated his conviction that for the 90 per cent of people who marry, life can be described as a two-act drama: 'Act one is the experience between the child and significant members of its family, and the second act is a repetition and further development of this experience in the marital relationship', because 'whenever we encounter an intimate affective relationship in life, we ultimately use all the emotional experiences learned in the first two decades of life'.

It follows that Dominian believes that the success of any marriage is enormously influenced by the ratio of good and bad experiences in the partners' childhoods, and by their successful negotiation of childhood's developmental tasks. If, for example, either partner's relationship with their parents was problematical or lacking in unconditional love, they may well, in his opinion, have difficulty in giving and receiving intimacy or emotional sustenance. Since most people arrive at marriage with a complex mixture of mature growth, unresolved conflicts and, occasionally, severe emotional wounds, he thinks that modern marriage is, almost by definition, a conflict-generating condition.

However, in recent years Dominian's analysis of the reasons for the enormous increase in the overall rate of divorce, as opposed to the causes of individual marital breakdown, has undergone a significant development. In *Passionate and Compassionate Love* he acknowledges that divorce is 'associated markedly with personality disorders', but then he states that these disorders 'are notoriously confusing entities in psychology and psychiatry' because there are different theoretical frameworks for classification. The framework that he himself has tended to use is a psychoanalytical one, which is largely Freudian and post-Freudian and 'depends on dynamic understanding of the growth of the personality'.

This approach which 'has as its basis sexuality, aggressions, feelings, emotions, affection and the capacity to form and sustain sexual and emotional relationships' has, in his opinion, been 'immensely productive' — indeed he asserts that 'modern counselling has been largely derived from dynamic psychology'. However, he has become increasingly aware of the negative repercussions that have resulted from its popularity: 'widespread counselling has unwittingly given the impression that those who divorce are essentially disturbed personalities', while marital breakdown has normally been analysed and explained on psychological grounds alone.

In fact, partly because of the influence of the sociologists he works with at his Marriage Research Centre, Dominian has recently undergone something of a conversion and now believes that 'the epidemic of divorce' is primarily rooted in 'powerful social forces producing historic changes in marriage'. Although he continues to stress that 'the personality plays a crucial role in the new dimensions of personal intimacy required by contemporary marriage', he has come to recognize that the fragility of 'contemporary marriage' derives first and foremost from the 'new dimensions' which arise from these 'powerful social forces', and only then from the 'psychological mechanisms which explain partially, only partially, the actual problems'. Indeed Dominian openly acknowledges that 'the failure to understand the social factors is a major defect in psychological thinking and I, as a psychiatrist, readily admit that I have been as blind as my colleagues'.

Dominian believes that there are two particularly important — and interrelated — social factors responsible for the 'historic changes in marriage': first and most decisively, the movement for the emancipation of women and its rapid acceleration in the last thirty years; secondly, the enormous increase in the partners' expectations of what marriage will offer. These factors have been responsible for bringing about a rapid re-orientation in the relationship of husband and wife from a 'task-orientated togetherness' to an 'interpersonal encounter of intimacy'. Whereas in a 'traditional role marriage', the basic model of marriage in the past, the husband was the principal income earner and the head of the family while his wife looked after the home and the children, in today's 'intimate relationship of love' the partners 'seek an equality of worth, a much greater flexibility in their complementary tasks, and emphasis on communication, demonstration of affection, sexual fulfilment and mutual realisation of potential'.

Dominian thinks these changes and the social factors responsible for them need to be seen in a proper historical perspective. Therefore, in *Marriage, Faith and Love* he traces the development of the family from the beginning of the modern era in 1550 until the watershed of the First World War. He follows the historian Lawrence Stone in dividing that period into three overlapping phases. In the first period, between 1550 and 1700, 'there was a marked tendency to patriarchy with a subordination of children to parents, and wife to husband'; the inception of marriage was left to the collective decision of the family while the filial role was one of obedience. In consequence, moral premises were very different from those of today. For example, there was thought to be nothing reprehensible about marriage for what Stone called 'interest' (money, status and power), rather than 'affect' (love, friendship and sexual attraction). On the contrary, 'romantic love and lust were strongly condemned as ephemeral and irrational grounds for marriage'.

Dominian believes that it was during the second phase, from about 1640 to 1800, that some of the features of the contemporary family first began to emerge: young people gained the right to choose their future spouse, although parents retained a veto; romantic love began to become a respectable motive for marriage; and there was an increased acceptance of 'affective individualism', the pursuit of happiness. Although patriarchy still dominated — Dominian quotes Blackstone: 'the husband and wife are one, and the husband is that one' — the increase in marital breakdown in the seventeenth and eighteenth centuries was, in his opinion, an indication of the same rising emotional expectations that have been partially responsible for a similar increase in recent years.

However, in the third phase, between 1800 and 1914, there was, according to Dominian, a return to the original outlook. Just as, during that first phase of the modern era, tension in society tended to make the home the place of safety and stability, 'so in the wake of the industrial revolution with its marked social change, the family became once again a citadel of entrenched hierarchical order'; children came once more under 'the discipline of the rod'; and there was intense repression of sexual activity in the upper socio-economic group. Dominian cites a well-known medical authority, Dr William Acton, maintaining in 1865 that the majority of women were happy not to be troubled by sexual feelings, while Mrs Ellis's advice to them in her book *The Daughters of England*, written 20 years earlier, was 'suffer and be still'! For the poor during this period, the whole focus of life, in Dominian's opinion, was narrowed down to a battle for survival.

Dominian thinks that the single most important cause of the change in the nature of marriage has been the movement for the emancipation of women. The initial catalyst was the contribution of women to the war effort between 1914 and 1918, followed in the inter-war period by a series of factors responsible for a slow increase in momentum between then and 1950. The aspirations of women in the upper socio-economic group, broadened in the war by their first experience of going out to work, were further enlarged by the subsequent expansion of educational facilities and the successful fight for the vote. At the same time, more and more women of all classes began to go out to work, thus gaining not only a degree of economic flexibility, but also the possibility of companionship, social identity, and a growth in self-confidence. Meanwhile, their freedom and independence had been increasing as the state gradually took over tasks which had previously been exclusively the concern of parents. Acts of Parliament, for example, ensured society's responsibility for universal education, while the introduction of the National Health Service after the Second World War meant that the care of serious illness could take place in hospital free of charge.

The 1950s and 1960s saw this movement of emancipation gather pace. Medical developments were of supreme importance. One advance was the decline in infant mortality. In *Marriage, Faith and Love*, Dominian cites statistics which show that this decline was a relatively recent phenomenon in England: out of every 1,000 live births in 1911, nearly 130 infants died; by 1982 the figure was 10.8. Another development of immense significance was the advent of reliable contraception. In *Make or Break* Dominian declared that 'since the early sixties, the advent of the contraceptive pill has produced a revolution in family life; widespread and safe birth regulation, now for the first time largely under the control of wives, means that childbearing has been brought under greater control than ever before'. As a result, women were frequently able not only to have the number of children they wanted, but also to have them when they wanted them. This was 'nothing less than a revolutionary enlargement of freedom', which, together with the decline in infant mortality, meant that whereas at the beginning of the century a working-class mother would spend about fifteen years of her life either pregnant or nursing a baby under the age of one, her modern equivalent would be similarly occupied for only four or five years.

Developments in the 1960s and 1970s were responsible for a significant change of mood in this movement. Dominian cites Simone de Beauvoir's *The Second Sex* (in English 1953), Germaine Greer's *The Female Eunuch* (1970), and Jill Tweedie's *In the Name of Love* (1979) as illustrations of powerful books which signalled a new militancy and 'another upsurge' in women's 'social, psychological, economic and legal emancipation'. Examples of this emancipation were the growing equality of opportunity of work and greater justice in property distribution, both of which helped to ensure fewer women were being forced by economic necessity to stay in marriages which had become unbearable.

Dominian believes that the second major reason for the change in the nature of marriage and the subsequent growth in the number and scale of marital difficulties has been the increase in the expectations of both partners. A fundamental element in this has been the rise in their life expectancy, an important criterion for the length of marriage, and another consequence of advances in curative and preventive medicine. In *Marriage, Faith and Love* he cites figures showing that the average length of first marriages among the poor in the late nineteenth century was 22 years; 'mortality of both sexes, and in particular of women during pregnancy and childbirth and in the post-puerperal period was the principal reason for this short duration.' By 1971 the average expectation of life at birth had increased to 68.6 years for men and 74.9 for women; the result is that marriages lasting 50 years 'are not unusual for contemporary society'.

The extra years that a husband and wife now have with each other are normally lived together in an environment far removed from the traditional preoccupation with procreation and the rearing of children. In addition, greater availability of housing has further increased their independence and privacy since it has ensured that parents and children can normally have separate homes. This availability is one example of the marked rise in living standards in the post-war era — a rise that has made it possible, in Dominian's opinion, for the challenges of food, shelter, employment, social security, education and health to be met to a considerable degree. Moreover, the reduction in the size of the average family has freed both parents from many child-orientated tasks, while technological advances have reduced working hours and made running a household easier.

Jack Dominian believes that when their basic needs of survival are met, there is a tendency for human beings in general — and for women in particular — to seek fulfilment at a deeper level of their being, the level of feelings, emotions and sexuality. Whereas in the past their energies were directed as they had been since time immemorial — outwardly towards survival — now the increase in leisure, freedom, independence and privacy in the lives of many couples has meant that 'task-oriented togetherness' has evolved into an 'interpersonal encounter of intimacy'.

This trend has coincided with and fed off another major development in the last half century — the emergence of psychology with its emphasis on that very inner world of 'feelings' and 'emotions' that is so central to any intimate relationship. As formal religion has evolved and, for many, receded into the background, so psychology has partially filled the vacuum. The ideas of Freud, Jung and Adler have penetrated widely into society and concepts such as 'instincts' and 'sexual drive' have become part of everyday thought and language. In addition, the increasing stress on sexuality has been accentuated by the publicity given to the studies of sexologists like Kinsey, and Masters and Johnson, which has further heightened the expectations most people have of both sex and marriage.

Dominian considers that all these different developments, and in particular the pronounced change in the role and status of women, have led to a new kind of man–woman relationship. It 'has changed in terms of equality and also in its emotional content; the result is much greater liberality in personal interaction with much greater emphasis on the presence and exchange of feelings'. Moreover, in this new type of relationship, 'women are likely to have an advantage over men' since they are better equipped for communication and for dealing with feelings. As a consequence 'the power between the sexes has had a redistribution with its axis shifting in the direction of wives'. Dominian believes that it is not a coincidence that seven out of ten divorce petitions are brought by women; increasingly they are not prepared to stay in a marriage that causes them harm or even in one that does not fulfil their expectations.

However it is not only women who have changed. Men's priorities now also often centre on the world of feelings, emotions and sexual fulfilment and they, too, seek emotional compatibility. It follows that the success of a modern marriage is much more dependent on the stability of both partners' personalities than it was previously, since these personalities are engaged at a much deeper level than before. Whereas in the past affective responses were kept strictly subordinate to social roles, now they play a crucial part in the relationship from its beginning and are normally expressed through 'a repertoire of previously learned behaviour'.

Because of the importance of both social and psychological factors, it is within a psycho-social framework that Jack Dominian has constructed a lifecycle for modern marriage. He has based this on the eight-stage process of E. E. Duval, but reduced it to a courtship phase, followed by three phases of marriage. Dominian firmly rejects the idea of marriage as an institution the essential features of which are static; rather, 'couples go through courtship and then become a married pair, have children whose growth spans two decades, and as they depart, the couple return to a one to one relationship'. The first phase of this cycle covers the first five years, from the average age of marriage (in 1981, 25.1 for men, 22.8 for women) to the late twenties or early thirties; the second phase, the years from the age of 30 to 50; and the third, the years from the age of 50 to the death of one spouse. In addition he believes that the marriage relationship has five main dimensions — social, emotional, sexual, intellectual and spiritual, each of which presents specific challenges in each phase.

During adolescence, young people are influenced by a number of social and psychological factors such as the experience of aloneness, and the desire for a home of their own and for the authority and status that marriage confers. This propels them towards 'falling in love' and 'coupling'. At the heart of 'falling in love' is physical attraction, based on a whole variety of factors among which are vision, touch and sound. 'Falling in love is a resuscitation of the physical and emotional links which form our primary emotional attachment to mother' — admittedly with the addition of an overall sexual dimension — 'and is a repeat in adult life of our infantile bonds.'

The other key components are emotional attraction and social fitness. Emotionally, there is a 'mutuality of significance' between the couple; 'when they meet each other, everybody else fades into insignificance.' Socially, 'we are usually attracted by people who are of the same intelligence and interests and share our values and opinions' — especially in social classes I and II. Dominian adds that some psychiatrists also postulate a theory of psychological similarity and complementarity — partners selecting each other because their unconscious feelings and emotions fit.

Those who have fallen in love are in a state of emotional excitement; they tend to idealize the person they love and desire closeness and contact. The features of the state include profound physiological arousal, difficulties in concentration and moments of intense jealousy. Love and romance are, in Dominian's opinion, the most powerful activators of our pleasure centres: 'both tend to be very exciting emotionally'; but 'if the relationship is not established securely or is uncertain, anxiety or other displeasure centres may be quite active as well, producing a state of great emotional turmoil, as the lover swings between hope and torment'.

'Falling in love' can lead to courtship. Theoretically, modern courtship is free from family and community pressures and offers an unlimited range of choice, yet, according to Dominian, studies in Britain and the USA have shown that spouses are normally chosen on the basis of 'assortative mating'. That is, they are drawn from people living in the same neighbourhood and possessing certain characteristics — similarity of age, social class, religion and education. However, although these social variables define the likely group of eligible people from whom the final choice will be made, as marital roles have become less rigid, so the most important criteria for courtship selection have become age and education rather than social class and religion. Dominian thinks that this trend makes the stability of marriage more and more dependent on the internal resources and cohesion of the spouses rather than the external supports provided by the community.

There have been two major developments in courtship in recent years: the rapidly increasing incidence of sexual intercourse and the escalation of cohabitation. Research in 1976, which Dominian cited in *Marriage, Faith and Love*, indicated that whereas 35 per cent of women married in 1959 and 1960 had had sexual intercourse with their husband before marriage, the figure had risen to 74 per cent of those married between 1971 and 1975; while in *Passionate and Compassionate Love* (1991), Dominian writes that 'today, almost everyone enters marriage having had sexual intercourse and increasingly couples cohabit for short or long periods'. Cohabitation is now the final stage of courtship for many couples, a development he thinks has been brought on by their alarm at the high divorce rate and their — false, in his opinion — belief that it will help confirm their partner's suitability.

Dominian considers courtship to be a process which normally lasts between one and two years, during which there is a constant checking and rechecking of attraction, suitability, complementarity and blending together: 'it is a vital time and the quality of the courtship is intimately linked with the outcome of the marriage.' He identifies four elements whose presence during courtship is associated with increased risk to the marriage: short courtships, stormy relationships, promiscuous behaviour and severe last-minute doubts about the future spouse.

Dominian believes that couples who marry after knowing each other for a few days or weeks are taking considerable risks. He recognizes that people can fall in love at first sight, but thinks 'this feeling needs to be tested in the course of a fuller experience'. Stormy relationships are also poor omens for the future; frequent arguments indicate 'that there is a basic difference of approach to something of importance and unless the conflict is resolved before the marriage, it is likely to continue afterwards'. Similarly he believes that if one partner leads a promiscuous life during court-ship, he or she will probably continue to do so during the marriage and must therefore be challenged about this behaviour before the wedding; otherwise the marriage will be very vulnerable. Finally Dominian distinguishes between last-minute anxiety about the wed-ding and about being married, and persistent anxieties about the future spouse. In general 'as long as there is no fundamental doubt about the partner, the marriage can proceed. But when the doubts are about the person, then caution should prevail.'

The first phase of the Dominian marital lifecycle covers the initial five years of marriage. In these vital years of adjustment, couples have to form a stable relationship in five different dimensions of life; three are of primary importance — the social, physical and emo-tional — and two secondary — the intellectual and the spiritual. The most important task in this phase is the transition from 'being in love' — that state of heightened emotional and sexual expecta-tion and idealization of the other — to 'loving', which he under-stands as involving an availability and a willingness to establish a minimum relationship in all those five dimensions. In this period the basic relationship of the partners needs to be established, but some never are; between 30 and 40 per cent of all marital break-downs occur in these first five years.

The social challenges facing a newly married couple normally include the evolution of relationships with parents, relatives and friends; the setting up of the home; the distribution of household tasks; agreement about finance; and the balancing of work and leisure. The most important of these is the separation of the spouses from their parents, and the fusion of a new unity as husband and wife. Sometimes one partner remains dependent on his or her parents, causing the other to feel excluded and not treated as a pro-per spouse. If requests to abandon this dependence are ignored and criticism follows, an alliance can be formed by parents and child against the other spouse, and the whole relationship endangered. At this stage parents tend to need their children, rather than vice versa, and often cross the thin line between support and intrusion. A similar and equally dangerous problem is when one partner is not approved of or is disliked by the other's family, which often causes a crisis of loyalty for their spouse.

The setting up of the home, the distribution of household tasks and agreement about finance are all possible sources of tension.

Despite increasing fluidity of roles with both partners working, Dominian thinks that husbands frequently don't pull their weight in the home and that a wife's subsequent exhaustion can kill both affection and sex. Similarly one partner's meanness, incompetence or extravagance with money often causes difficulties. Money possesses a strong emotional component as well as symbolizing power, and a wife kept short of it feels unloved. However, although household issues are potentially divisive, they are less dangerous than the situation in which a young couple have to share a home with either partner's parents, or with somebody else. In *An Introduction to Marital Problems*, Dominian cites research findings that those couples who start married life in this way have a greater tendency to marital breakdown than those who start with their own home.

The three other 'social' challenges involve work, leisure and friends. The two problems associated with work are contrasting ones; both long hours and the devastating effect on self-esteem wrought by unemployment can, in Dominian's opinion, reduce emotional availability. Leisure also presents two very different dangers. One partner, more often than not the husband, may continue to live his leisure time like a bachelor. Alternatively one spouse can try to restrict the other's freedom, expecting their partner to give up all their leisure pursuits and remain at home; he or she often feels trapped or imprisoned as a result. The issue of friends is linked to that of leisure; just as parents can intrude, so some friends may remain so central in one spouse's life that their presence or influence is resented by their partner who feels jealous, or one spouse may have a wide circle of friends, the other only a few, and the lonely partner can try to detach and isolate their spouse.

Physically, the major requirement in these early years is a degree of sexual satisfaction. Dominian believes that in the past, when the social structure of marital roles rather than the emotional and sexual content of their relationship was emphasized, deficiencies in a couple's sexual life might well have been accepted without complaint. Now with expectations of personal and sexual fulfilment so high, sexual disappointment can be a significant cause of a break-up. He thinks that it normally takes about a year for those couples who haven't cohabited previously to settle to a satisfactory rhythm of sexual life, and that two particular types of problem surface in this period: difficulties of what Dominian calls 'function', and poor quality of experience. Although difficulties in function — in terms of adequate sex drive, potency, and frequency of intercourse and ejaculation for the man, and the capacity to be penetrated and to enjoy sex without pain on the part of the woman — are now understood better than they were and can more easily be referred to a specialist unit for help, Dominian cites statistics which suggest that between 12 and 18 per cent of marriages still encounter problems in the first five years.

The more dangerous situation is when the quality of the experience is poor. Dominian stresses that there is much more involved in sexual satisfaction than obtaining an orgasm. He considers foreplay to be particularly important as it is an opportunity for the couple to make it very clear to each other that they are recognized, wanted and appreciated as spouses. Indeed, good communication is necessary throughout the whole experience of lovemaking. Such communication includes making one's partner aware of areas which are pleasurable, the quality of touch that is desired, the degree of arousal necessary prior to genital entry, and the type of physical exchange required to produce a satisfactory orgasm. If this communication is limited, the foundations of discontent may be laid for a husband to feel sexually deprived, or a wife to feel she is treated as a sexual object rather than as a person.

Sexual intercourse is important, but it is not the only form of emotional communication. Emotional communication — that is, the conveying of each partner's inner needs to the other and the reassessment of their mutual understanding — has, in all its forms, a central place in the relationship of the spouses in this and every phase. In *Passionate and Compassionate Love* Dominian suggests four situations involving the emotions which can lead to difficulties in this initial phase.

The first situation is the loss of idealization, however necessary. During the falling-in-love stage a couple are held together by a deep idealization of each other. When they are hit by the reality of their partner's limitations — be they social defects, or emotional shortcomings like an incapacity to feel or be affectionate — profound disillusionment can set in and lead to thoughts like 'this is not the person I fell in love with'. Secondly, some newly married individuals find it very difficult to cope with the restraints marriage or their partner imposes on their freedom of movement. This can connect with the third factor, an inability to cope with intimacy. Although an individual who has this difficulty may overcome it during courtship, the continuous physical and emotional closeness can become intolerable for them. Finally, in these early years of marriage what Dominian calls 'immaturity' may surface; loss of temper, excessive drinking, aggression, poor work record, and possessiveness are symptoms which gradually reveal this reality to a spouse. In addition to these situations, those relationships which are 'particularly egalitarian' face two extra challenges — the distribution of power and the resolution of conflict. These problems are more likely to surface in the higher socio-economic groups because their way of relating is less patriarchal, and every major decision has therefore to be reached on the basis of consensus.

Among these major decisions is that of when to try to have the first child. In *Marriage, Faith and Love* Dominian cites statistics suggesting that whereas 15 per cent of those married between 1955 and 1959 had a baby in their first year of marriage and 45 per cent in the second year, by the mid-1970s the percentage had declined to 9 per cent and 26 per cent. He believes that the norm today is for the first child to be born towards the end of this first phase of five years. Whenever it happens, it causes a drastic upheaval, a massive change in the social and psychological structure of the home and, frequently, 'a psycho-social crisis'. The wife becomes a mother and normally leaves work. The husband becomes a father and has to support his wife and child emotionally and economically. The baby requires attention from both spouses. This affection is withdrawn from their partner. Fatigue increases greatly and can seriously affect emotional and sexual communication. Dominian thinks that if there was already tension in the marital relationship, the birth of the child is likely to accentuate it.

The second phase in the Dominian marital lifecycle spans the two decades between the ages of 30 and 50. He views it as a period characterized by children being born, growing up and beginning to depart from home; by the husband's career taking a decisive turn and the wife often returning to work; and, frequently, by a change of awareness and personality on the part of one spouse the response to which is fundamental to the survival of the marriage. Dominian believes that it is during this second phase that the challenges of maintaining the marital relationship are most acute and that most break-ups occur.

In the social dimension, the central focus is the work performance of the spouses, particularly the husband, although increasingly the wife's career matters. Some specific situations are likely to cause problems. One spouse, normally the husband, may become unemployed, be disappointed in his expectations or rise to a level

beyond his capabilities. Alternatively, he may be almost too successful and upwardly socially mobile for the good of the marriage. Each
of these situations can put strain on the relationship. Unemployment's shattering effect on self-esteem is particularly damaging for
a person who lacks confidence in his personal relationships and relies
on work for his identity and sense of self-worth. If his partner fails
to reassure him that he matters through affection, sex and encouragement, the marriage can be at risk. Dominian states in *Passionate
and Compassionate Love* that there is good evidence that unemployment increases the incidence of marriage breakdown. Paradoxically,
the opposite experience is also potentially dangerous: a successful
husband can have less time for his family or lose touch with his wife;
and upward social mobility frequently leads to the trauma of moving
house, an upset that tends to affect a wife more than a husband,
particularly if the latter's prime source of emotional meaning is his
work. In general, any impermanence in the social network tends to
operate against stability — as when one spouse's new friends or colleagues alienate the other.

A second area of possible tension in the social and emotional
dimension is caused by the advent of children. As has been mentioned, the first child is normally born at the end of the first or the
beginning of this second phase. After its birth, a mother's health
is vulnerable — post-puerperal depression, in particular, can cause
havoc. However the fundamental challenge after the birth of a
child is to find the right balance between being a parent and being
a spouse. As Dominian states in *Passionate and Compassionate Love*,
'counsellors hear repeatedly the story of the mother who was so preoccupied with the children that she neglected the needs of her husband. Equally the husband who neglects his wife when the children
are growing up is a constant complaint on the lips of wives. Neglected husbands have affairs and marriages break up unnecessarily.'

Moreover, children can accentuate the problems by their own
behaviour. The classic example is the triangular situation postulated
by Freud, who asserted that children, frequently from very early in
their life, offer a reciprocated affection first for one parent and then
for the other, which causes an inherent splitting and sundering apart,
and that this can increase as they grow older and are able more
consciously to play their parents off against each other. Dominian believes that the onset of puberty and adolescence are especially
difficult for parents, and often lead to anxiety, tension and disagreement as to the best way to handle situations. In his opinion, it is a

real danger for a marriage if parents feel their children must come
first at all times and neglect being alone with each other and going
out together. They need to take trouble to preserve their love and
sexuality for each other, since their children are best served when
they do not forget their own needs.

Physically, health can begin to deteriorate and disease may strike
in this phase, but it is sexual satisfaction that remains the key
feature. In *Marriage, Faith and Love* Dominian cites statistics from his
Marriage Research Centre to the effect that marital happiness is
closely related to sexual satisfaction. The study *Who Divorces?* found
that in a stably married population, 96 per cent of women and 98
per cent of men claimed that the sexual side of their marriage had
either started and continued satisfactorily, or that earlier difficulties
had been resolved, whereas 38 per cent of divorced women and 30
per cent of divorced men whose initial sexual relationship had been
good stated that it had deteriorated. Dominian believes that this is
the phase when sexual problems are most likely to come to the fore,
and that these problems are more likely to be the result of an
unsatisfactory attitude of the type that emerged in the first phase
— such as lack of affection and lack of preparation for intercourse — than of sexual dysfunction.

Dominian also refers to another type of 'difficulty' which is very
frequent in this phase — infidelity. He believes that if marriages in
which affairs have happened are to be saved, the 'innocent' partner
must seek to understand the conscious and, as far as possible, the
unconscious unmet emotional and sexual needs of the partner who
had the affair, and then try to meet them.

However, Dominian is clear that it is within the emotional dimension of this second phase that the biggest single challenge in contemporary marriage is to be found — in the form of a major shift from
emotional dependence to independence on the part of one of the
spouses. It is not unusual for one partner, normally the wife, to
begin marriage by treating her husband as an extension of a powerful
parental figure, looking to him for guidance, clarification and
decision-making; then, imperceptibly, to begin to build up her
self-confidence, frequently through children or work, to live life more
and more on the basis of her own evaluations and decisions and so to
discover and 'possess' herself. In *Make or Break* Dominian quotes as
a typical example of this process the woman who said in counselling:
'All my life I have done what others want me to do. First it was
my parents and then my husband. Now I want to do what I want.'

Dominian believes that in these circumstances the fate of the marriage depends on the reaction of the partner. If he begins to see the change in his wife at an early stage and encourages it, the shift can proceed smoothly and advantageously for both spouses and enable a new level of mutual autonomy to emerge. However, if he sees her growth as a threat and tries to block her initiatives, frequently she will become angry and he, in return, increasingly anxious, afraid and confused.

This movement from dependence to independence can be accompanied or followed by a similar shift from insecurity to security; as the previously dependent partner withdraws from the influence of her spouse she begins to evaluate life from her own point of view and to clarify her own identity. This gradual removal of external influences and the acceptance of self as belonging to self frequently leads to a growth in self-esteem. As Dominian observed in *Marriage, Faith and Love*: 'The transformation of Pinocchio was from a wooden toy to a real boy; the transformation of each one of us is from a delegated existence and worth to self-acceptance and the possession of a lovable self.'

The partner who has changed has been used to giving recognition and appreciation; now she wants to receive it. This reversal of their normal emotional exchange can utterly disorientate a couple. Such change and the confusion that goes with it is a recurring experience and can be disastrous for a marriage. Dominian describes a standard scenario as one in which one partner who may have been anxious, frightened or guilty at the start of the relationship, and who has taken years to gain her independence and self-esteem, begins to recognize that it is to her disadvantage to continue to behave as an underdog. When she asserts herself, she frequently finds that she has to work through the onslaught of her spouse who makes her feel either bad or mad because of her new approach. In the course of all this, she grows so angry that the relationship totally disintegrates. So frequently has Dominian come across this kind of situation and so powerless has he experienced a counsellor to be in these circumstances that in *Passionate and Compassionate Love* he several times recommends the examination of marriages at regular intervals so that any such changes might be recognized at an early enough stage to prevent the break-up of the relationship.

Changes in the intellectual and spiritual dimensions in this phase are related to these changes in the emotional dimension. The deeper layers of the personality often seek expression as couples begin to relate with parts of themselves that were hitherto undeveloped, unaccepted or unconscious. Outlook, opinions and attitudes often alter. A husband, for example, may become less concerned with success at work and concentrate more on relationships; and either partner's faith, if not effectively integrated into their developing personality, may become meaningless and be discarded. Dominian thinks that any changes in one spouse have to be congruent and acceptable to the other, if harmony is to be retained in their relationship. Otherwise, as he described in *Passionate and Compassionate Love*, 'the specific contribution of this period' will be 'the marked bitterness and vehemence' of the emancipating partner and the anxiety of her spouse 'who often has little idea what is happening and is petrified of losing his partner'.

The third phase in the Dominian marital lifecycle covers the period from the age of 50 to the death of one spouse. This period may last twenty or thirty years or more and is something new in human history, the product of modern health and medical advances. In these years children leave home and marry, grandchildren are born, and the couple return to a one-to-one relationship, facing each other alone again and ultimately having to endure illness and death. Dominian cites studies which suggest that in this phase marital satisfaction — which started falling soon after the wedding and declined appreciably when children were born — begins to rise again; yet, paradoxically, the second peak period for marital breakdown occurs around the beginning of this period, after 20 to 25 years of marriage.

The social dimension of life in this phase normally focuses on the husband's work situation, the illness and death of the couple's parents, and the marriage of their children. Whereas workers in the lower socio-economic groups have reached their peak much earlier, for many in the professional and managerial classes this is the time either for the end of their promotion hopes, or for redundancy and early retirement; frequently this increases the demands on the wife, since she more than anyone can restore lost confidence. During this phase responsibilities for children are often replaced by responsibilities for elderly parents and for grandchildren. This still leaves a greater freedom than previously, which is further increased by the retirement of both partners, although that brings its own particular challenges.

Emotionally, the main phenomenon is the situation brought about by the departure of the children and the return to what Dominian refers to as 'the dyad state'. So much depends on whether the couple have retained a meaningful relationship. If they have, it is a phase with enormous potential for the revitalization of intimacy. Dominian, following Jung, speculates that for many couples this can be a time when a synthesis of opposites takes place. If the relationship is good, this psychological integration of opposites can result in a much greater understanding and empathy between the spouses, since they have conscious access to the whole of their personalities and their integrated selves can now meet each other. As a consequence, this period frequently witnesses new harmony and enjoyment, with an increase in companionship, a sharing of leisure activities, and mutual pleasure in married children and grandchildren.

However, this phase can also be a time when the spouse is discovered to be a stranger. Often that is because couples have lived their lives in parallel, she the child-bearer and rearer, he the provider. Moreover the stranger can be someone with whom one finds one has little in common. In these circumstances, separation and divorce frequently follow. Dominian cites figures which suggest that one in five of marriages that break up do so at this point, the main reason usually being the emotional and sexual separation that existed long before the children's departure. When the alienation is mutual, there is little pain involved, but if one partner is still emotionally attached, there can be great distress. Moreover, as Dominian comments in *Make or Break*, break-ups at this phase 'do not offer as many opportunities for prevention' as those that occur in the early years of marriage.

There are two other sources of possible problems in the emotional dimension of this phase. The emotional transformation that so often takes place in the second phase can also occur in this one. Some people who failed to be rebellious or independent or to enjoy themselves in their youth can reach a kind of emotional adolescence in their fifties. They may then appear to their confused spouse and children to be behaving irresponsibly although they themselves feel that in the emotional realization of the characteristics of youth they are recapturing a lost first spring of life. More frequently, as this phase goes on there is a gradual reversal of the roles of parent–child dependence. Parents become emotionally and sometimes materially dependent on their children, especially in the years leading up to the death of one of the spouses.

Physically, the phase usually opens with the wife's menopause. This can cause emotional difficulties but normally has no adverse consequences for her sexual life unless it has been poor for some time. If that has been the case, the menopause is often used as an excuse for bringing sexual activity between the couple to a close. In general, however, their sexual life tends to continue with reduced incidence, but with a significant degree of continuity and enjoyment. Indeed, Dominian thinks that after the menopause some women seem to come very much alive sexually and that the main threat to an active sexual life is, in fact, male impotence, which Kinsey and later studies have shown rises in a cumulative manner during these decades.

Extra-marital affairs continue to occur during this period. Dominian cites one American study in which half of those husbands whose children had left home expressed a desire for such an affair and a quarter actually had relationships. The main causes are similar to those of affairs in the previous phase — mid-life crisis anxiety and the need for reassurance that one is still sexually attractive. In addition, delayed emotional development can be a factor. In *An Introduction to Marital Problems* Dominian cites clinical evidence which suggests that frequently it is the husband rather than the wife who is the late developer. Sometimes, having persevered through a sense of duty and loyalty over two decades, he gradually becomes aware that his choice of wife was not an independent one but was influenced by his parents or by his desire to marry, and so he decides to have an affair or to leave his wife. This situation is especially difficult for his spouse, who finds her husband's behaviour as incomprehensible as it is painful.

Finally, in this phase, Dominian believes that the intellectual and spiritual dimensions of life tend to become more prominent. As material needs are met or appear less important, knowledge can mature into wisdom and the spiritual become more significant. Although 'there are many other urgent priorities which dilute the intensity of this quest' some men and women start 'second journeys' in which their aim is service, rather than monetary or material gain, while in others there is an increasing quest for the meaning of life and sometimes a desire to withdraw from the world.

Jack Dominian divides the marital lifecycle into courtship and three distinct phases because he views marriage as 'a dynamic unfolding process with its own distinctive features in each phase'. He considers that 'the viability of marriage depends on the continuing realisation at a minimum level' of its social, intellectual, emotional, physical and spiritual dimensions. Although some conflicts between spouses cause hurts which are quickly forgotten, others can endanger an essential part of a person's humanity and lead to dissatisfaction at the core of their being. Ultimately if a spouse's essential needs of love are not being met, or if they are the victim of unacceptable behaviour, the marriage is in danger. As a consequence, in *Passionate and Compassionate Love* he singles out for particular examination two specific areas — sexual difficulties and infidelity — even though the problems they cause have been addressed in each phase.

Dominian believes that in recent years there has been a marked alteration in attitudes to sexuality. Evidence from various sources indicates that it is women who are changing and now 'want to experience sex in its full meaning with a mutuality of satisfaction and fulfilment'. This development is linked with two other changes which have added to the importance of sex in marriage. The first is the availability of widespread contraception which has ensured that the overwhelming majority of acts of sexual intercourse in marriage are non-procreative. As a consequence, he thinks, couples are seeking a new meaning for their sexuality, and in this search the wife is as important and active as her husband. The second, which also results from the severing of the link between sexual intercourse and procreation, is the reduction in the average size of the family. In an unpublished paper, 'Marital breakdown in the light of changing sexual attitudes', Dominian concludes that 'sex, affection and an egalitarian relationship are the principal factors which provide the infrastructure of a contented marriage', and suggests that 'if that be the case, then we have to pay infinitely more attention to the quality of sexual intercourse in marriage, and in particular identify the broad patterns of disturbance'.

In *Passionate and Compassionate Love* Dominian places these 'patterns of disturbance' in their psychological and sociological context, which is that childhood is the first intimate relationship of personal love and marriage the second. If there were problems in the personal dimension in that first intimate relationship, he believes they will reappear in the second and may focus on the sexual act, since it is there that the personal meets the erotic.

The most common psychologically rooted problem in this area affects the man or woman who has been emotionally deprived in childhood and experienced the feeling of not being loved, wanted or appreciated. One consequence can be that he or she feels used and not loved during sex, and so fails to enjoy it. Alternatively, he

or she can seek to satisfy their own emotional needs by a high frequency of lovemaking. Husbands are particularly prone to using sex
as a substitute for affection when they find it difficult to reach their
wife emotionally. Similarly, a spouse who feels neglected can use
sex as a way of exercising power over their partner and so alienate
him or her at a personal level.

Social factors can also cause sexual problems, particularly among
women. Dominian cites three defective attitudes that he believes are
caused by particular types of upbringing: that sex is for having
children and therefore that once the desired size of family has been
reached there is no more need for sexual intercourse; that sex is for
men and that all women have to do is please them; and that sex
is dirty and a cause for guilt. All these attitudes will obviously lead
to difficulties in relationships.

Just as a couple may have difficulties at a personal level which
are socially and psychologically based and which prevent them from
wanting or enjoying sex, so they may also be hampered by difficulties at the 'erotic' level. Dominian considers the erotic dimension to comprise desire, arousal, intercourse and 'the aftermath'.
Female desire is closely linked to mood — so the background relationship is normally more important for the woman than a man; but
even if the relationship and mood are right, the phase of arousal still
has to be taken seriously if the woman is going to be fully involved.
'The success of intercourse is obtained when the personal and the
erotic are in tune and fuse with one another.'

Dominian emphasizes that sexual difficulties can exist in a good
relationship. However he also thinks that one of the effects of
a deterioration in the personal relationship between two partners
is infrequent, unsatisfactory or absent sex. Sexual difficulties are
often the consequence of one or both spouses becoming emotionally
detached or falling out of love and so can be a symptom rather than
a cause of the problem. A relationship initially based on one partner's need for security or dependence but in which those needs have
been outgrown is particularly prone to sexual difficulties.

He also examines three other problem areas: sexual abuse, sexual
dysfunctions, and the loss of sexual interest. Sexual abuse as a child
leaves its scars on an adult and means sex can be associated with
exploitation rather than love; a sensitive partner can heal the wound,
an indifferent one confirm the anticipated dread, with very negative repercussions for the relationship. The main sexual dysfunctions are non-consummation, which Dominian thinks affects about

1 per cent of couples; premature ejaculation and impotence on the part of the male; dyspareunia, the experience of pain during sexual intercourse, and anorgasmia, the failure to have an orgasm, on the part of the woman. These frequently have a psychological as well as a physiological base and require specialist help in the form of sexual therapy. The most common biological reason for a loss of interest in sex is post-puerperal depression. Up to 80 per cent of mothers suffer from 'maternal blues' and recover quickly, but 10 per cent who start their depression a week or so after giving birth can remain depressed for a considerable time, and in the process cease to enjoy sex. Dominian believes that explains why so many couples giving an account of their marital difficulties pinpoint the aftermath of the birth of one of their children as the starting-point of their problems.

Jack Dominian suggests in *Passionate and Compassionate Love* that up to 50 per cent of married men and women may indulge in an episode of infidelity. There and in several of his other books, he analyses the different types of infidelity, the reasons for them, and the responses required by the 'innocent party' if the affair is not seriously to threaten a marriage.

He believes that there are three main categories of infidelity, each with a different emotional and sexual meaning. The first is the one-night stand, a purely physical exchange in which two people, who find each other attractive, have sex. Dominian views it as a clear violation of human integrity since there is no personal dimension, but one which need not threaten a marriage in any way. The second type is a transient infidelity which may last for months or years, but which is not intended to break up a marriage; in this type of relationship, everyone is cheated. The third category is when an extramarital relationship is an indication of a serious threat to a marriage; often the marriage is already considered over, and the affair is entered into as a potential replacement for it. This, in Dominian's opinion, is the final betrayal of the other partner. Sometimes, however, an individual is unclear in himself or herself whether the affair is of the second or third variety and cannot make up their mind whether to return or to leave the marriage. Children, guilt and obligation often compete with the heart and a greater emotional and physical attraction, which leads to 'confusion, uncertainty, heated arguments and a lot of stress'.

The cause of many affairs is sexual attraction, combined with boredom and the seeking of excitement of the furtive, secretive variety. However, emotional reasons can also be important; moreover, affairs can have positive aspects in terms of personal and sexual self-esteem, even if 'the gain is attained at a price of pain, cheating, betrayal, loss of trust, and the difficulty in maintaining two relationships'. Dominian cites, as examples of gain, the emotionally deprived spouse who never gets enough love from their partner and seeks and finds some extra attention in an affair, and those spouses who have extramarital affairs of some duration in order to seek parts of themselves that are not being experienced within their marriage.

Dominian then examines the effect of infidelity on a marriage. In general, since mutual trust has been breached, severe difficulties result. The extent of the trauma depends on which category the affair belongs to. If the affair was a casual one a couple will normally, but not always, come to terms with it. However 'some men and women are more vulnerable and find any extramarital activity intolerable; they are often men and women with insecure attachments who are readily threatened by the possibility of loss, and an affair however trivial, is considered by them to be a serious change in the relationship'. Dominian thinks that their lack of forgiveness can be as responsible as the original affair for causing their spouse to abandon the marriage.

As has been mentioned Dominian has definite views as to the necessary response to a partner's infidelity. More is needed than forgiveness. He believes it important that the 'innocent' party examine their conscience to search out their own contribution to the infidelity, analysing in what way they might have been partially responsible through emotional or sexual neglect of their spouse. However he accepts that a person who indulges in numerous extramarital affairs is liable to have a personality disorder and will often require professional help, since 'very often such men and women are extremely insecure people with low self-esteem, who need to be reassured repeatedly that they are wanted and appreciated'.

Finally, Dominian addresses the issue of whether a spouse who has committed adultery should tell their partner. 'If this is directed towards the improvement of the relationship, then it has a justification. If it is meant to achieve an assuagement of guilt feeling . . . then clearly nothing will be gained except the infliction of pain on the partner. This pain is only justified when it can lead to a positive development of the relationship.'

CHAPTER SIX

The causes and consequences of divorce

The year that Jack Dominian began counselling for CMAC, 1958, was the year of the lowest post-war divorce rate in the United Kingdom, one-seventh of the present figure. Since then, divorce has rapidly escalated in the whole of Western society; in 1960, there were 25,000 divorces in England and Wales, in 1990, 150,000. The extent of the social upheaval involved is indicated by the number of people directly affected by marital breakdown each year. In 1980 it was estimated that the average number of children per divorcing couple in the United Kingdom under the age of sixteen was 1.12; with the rise in the divorce rate since then, Dominian thinks that approximately 500,000 'new' men, women and children each year — and therefore five million each decade — suffer directly from its consequences. In line with the latest research, he also estimates that 40 per cent of current marriages in the United Kingdom are heading for dissolution.

Jack Dominian's explanation for the modern epidemic of divorce was presented in part in the last chapter. He believes that 'there are powerful social forces producing historic changes' in personal relationships 'coupled with rising expectations, and that the gap between these rapid changes and an effective response has been filled by divorce'. A 'global transformation' of outlook has been brought about by such developments as the emancipation of women and the advent of Freud and dynamic psychology, so that the accent in marriage is now on sexuality and affectivity, transmitted by affirmation and communication, with both partners expecting to be engaged and understood at a deep level of their personality. If either feels their minimum needs in these areas are not being met, the marriage is in danger.

This has meant, according to Dominian, that modern marriage

has become a dynamic and shifting affair, within which there are several phases. During each of these phases, the couple have to negotiate developmental challenges in three main dimensions, the emotional, the social and the sexual. In his presentation of the marital lifecycle Dominian has shown that if either partner fails to respond to these challenges a marriage is liable to founder.

In addition to these two main causes for the increase in the divorce rate — the global transformation of outlook with its effect on expectations and the failure to respond to the psycho-social developmental challenges in the different phases of marriage — Dominian identifies certain psychological and sociological characteristics whose presence indicate that a marriage is potentially vulnerable. These characteristics are youthful marriages, premarital pregnancies, lack of assortative mating and belonging to a low socio-economic class.

Dominian states in *Make or Break* that 'studies from all over the world have shown that marriages under the age of twenty carry a high risk of future marital dissolution'. The problem is not necessarily youthfulness as such, but the social and emotional immaturity associated with it. Although emotional immaturity doesn't impair fecundity or a capacity for work — central to the old 'instrumental' model of marriage — it does hamper the encounter of personalities and the search for mutual understanding at an emotional level which is at the heart of the new model. Individuals in their late teens can be close to physical and even intellectual maturity but their emotional growth is far from complete. Moreover, youthful marriages are associated with housing, work and economic disadvantages. The combination of these disadvantages and emotional difficulties may be too great a burden for a young couple to cope with.

Premarital or early pregnancy and the arrival of a child in the first months of a marriage have also been shown to be linked to high divorce rates. Such a beginning to married life puts constraints on a couple and especially on the wife, and can make her feel resentful and frustrated, while the presence of a baby may divert the partners' attention from each other, hindering the formation in those early years of the strong bond that is so important for the future stability of their relationship. In addition, as Dominian suggests somewhat tendentiously in *Marriage, Faith and Love*, 'those with premarital pregnancies tend to have a higher sexual drive before and during marriage and extramaritally. This suggests a personality profile tending towards an extrovert make-up with a certain compulsion towards high sexual activity with shallow relationships.'

Sociologists, says Dominian, have 'established with some certainty that in the seeking of a partner, the field of eligibles is scanned
and assortative mating takes place, that is, like marries like'. Dominian thinks that there is considerable evidence that when similarity —
in education, social background, age, financial position, race or
religion — is ignored, the risk of divorce rises. The explanation is
straightforward: 'the viability of the relationship needs a certain
amount of similarity in all these areas. If barriers are crossed in these
social factors, there is an added strain which may be the last straw.'

The fourth potentially damaging characteristic is the social class
of the couple. Dominian writes in *Make or Break* that there is a clear
inverse relationship between social class and divorce: the lower the
socio-economic group, the higher the risk of divorce — although
'studies in Britain have also indicated that Class III non-manual is
also vulnerable'. The high rate of marital breakdown in the lowest
socio-economic group, in his opinion, may be a reflection of the combination of youthful marriages, immaturity, premarital pregnancies
and housing and economic difficulties.

One other psychosocial factor indicates a potentially fragile relationship: if one or both partners have been married before. In *Make
or Break* Dominian states that 80 per cent of all those who divorce
under the age of 30 will remarry. However, whereas 'it used to be
thought that remarriages were more stable than first marriages',
recent research suggests that second marriages are even more
vulnerable than first ones. Although some factors that might have
been causes of the break-up of the first marriage — such as extreme
youthfulness or a premarital pregnancy — are unlikely to be present
in a second one, personal psychological difficulties tend to retain
their destructive potential. For example, some individuals who are
extraordinarily sensitive and feel criticized and rejected at the drop
of a hat will carry that sensitivity into second and subsequent relationships, while others' sexual skills and capacity for sexual enjoyment will always be poor. Furthermore, children from previous
marriages may cause additional problems.

Dominian's counselling experience suggests to him that a second
marriage is liable to fail unless the individual has some understanding of the reasons for the break-up of the first relationship: 'A great
deal of care is needed to get insight into one's own real needs
and ensure that the second spouse is not unconsciously chosen
on the basis of needs which will repeat the difficulties of the first.'

In 1984 Jack Dominian addressed a conference on 'Marriage,

Divorce and the Family' arranged by his Marriage Research Centre. He optimistically described marital breakdown as 'a grinding of gears as society moves to a higher level of realisation of human potential through interpersonal relationships', asserting that the evidence pointed to divorce being a sign on the way in the search for a new model of marriage. He suggested that since 'the movement is in the direction of greater human fulfilment', the main need was 'to respond positively to the challenge'.

One of the reasons Dominian felt able to be so optimistic was his belief that a major reason for the rapid increase in the divorce rate has been the speed at which the 'historic changes' have taken place. In his opinion, there has been no time 'for proper assessment, evaluation and effective educational and supportive measures to respond to this changing situation'. However, the reverse side of Dominian's faith in the potential of education to combat marital breakdown is his tendency to seek scapegoats because of the failure so far to 'solve the problem'. He identifies the Church and society as particularly guilty in this respect.

Dominian believes that 'the basic Christian background of western societies is particularly weak in its understanding and handling of the subjects of sex and women'. As a result 'the churches have proved to be severely impotent in grasping and responding to these changes'. Although he acknowledges that 'in its recent thought, the main Christian Churches have identified the link between marriage and love, and have eloquently described it', he thinks there is a great need for them 'to put flesh on this insight'.

Dominian also asserts that society in general has signally failed to respond to the challenge of the enormous increase in marital breakdown and indeed that it has been mesmerized by the phenomenon of divorce. Although the initial thrust of divorce reform was to give relief to those who were unhappily married, he believes the consequence of this was that the effects of marital breakdown were minimized. As a result, society's only practical response to the problem has been a negative one — the passing of laws that have made divorce easier to obtain. Partly as a consequence of this, divorce has become socially and morally acceptable, since, as so often, morality has followed law.

The Divorce Reform Act in England and Wales, through which 'irretrievable breakdown of marriage' became the sole ground of petitioning, was promulgated in 1969 and was followed by the 1984 Family Proceedings Act, which made it possible for these petitions to be presented to a court after one rather than three years of marriage. In *Sexual Integrity* Dominian stated that there was little doubt in his mind that these legal changes in Britain meant effectively that 'the law offers no protection whatever to the stability of marriage'.

Jack Dominian is as aware of the consequences of marital breakdown as he is of its causes. In *God, Sex and Love* he suggests that no one person sees the complete havoc wrought by divorce: 'the doctor sees the stress symptoms associated with marital conflict; the hospital the consequences in alcohol consumption, affective disorders, suicidal attempts, suicides and general disease; the teacher sees the adverse consequences on children in their behaviour at school; the clergy the immense moral dilemmas posed by divorce; the magistrate the results of juvenile delinquency; the solicitor the unhappiness and anger of frustrated spouses; and society picks up the bill for nearly two billion pounds a year as a cost of marital breakdown.'

Dominian recognizes that it is particularly difficult to assess the effects of marital breakdown and divorce on a couple when so many of these are unquantifiable. However, he believes the break-up of any marriage is 'a betrayal of some of the deepest aspirations of the human spirit' and 'a nail in the coffin of human love'. Whatever the spouses' attitude at the time of the dissolution, there will inevitably be some erosion in the conviction and trust that human love is possible, and, as a result, the growth of a certain cynicism. In addition, he thinks that although the need for pairing is so powerful that a high percentage of divorcees remarry, second and third marriages do not, as a rule, have the clarity and conviction of motivation present in the first relationship. They are 'forged much more on a combination of reality and the possible than on the richness of sacrificial first love which engages the deeper elements of the personality'.

Dominian believes it is important to see divorce in context. Marriages do not normally break down suddenly. Frequently there is a recognizable pattern of events and emotions in the months before and after a separation; there is evidence for example that marital and family difficulties are the most common reason for women, and the second most common reason for men, to consult their doctors. As tension in the family rises, it is often accompanied by drinking bouts and episodes of aggression and depression. When separation becomes a real possibility, anxiety mounts. As it becomes a reality this anxiety develops into a host of physical and physiological symptoms suggestive of a deep inner sadness. In the immediate post-separation period, this sadness reveals itself in a variety of forms:

weeping, increased drinking and smoking, poor sleep and appetite, loss of energy and weight and sometimes even a suicide attempt. Occasionally one or both partners are relieved to be freed from a situation of great stress but the much more usual reaction is a lengthy period of grieving, persisting for months, and even years.

Dominian agrees with recent research that indicates that what happens to the partners after their separation depends, in the long term, on whether they remain single or marry again. There is strong evidence that those who remain unattached are prey both to psychological illness, with a higher than average degree of referral to outpatient departments and admission to psychiatric units, and to physical ill-health, with an increased likelihood of cancer or heart disease, or a serious accident. He cites studies from several countries which have shown that the rate of suicide for the unattached divorcee is many times higher than the average for the population as a whole. One such study suggests that the suicide rate per 100,000 of the population is 7.8 for the married, 35.5 for the divorced, and 204.4 for the separated person living alone. Dominian concludes that the individual who is divorced and remains unattached is a very vulnerable person, physically and psychologically.

However Dominian does not think that the outlook for those who remarry is significantly more promising. He cites recent research that suggests that although cohabitation is becoming an increasingly popular alternative, a high percentage of divorced people marry again, but that, as has been indicated, second marriages have a higher failure rate than first ones. It follows that many individuals will suffer the agonies of separation and divorce more than once.

The nature of the impact of divorce on children has been a hotly debated issue, partly because until recently there was a dearth of research on the subject. However, in the last few years, more and more evidence has become available, almost all of it revealing the negative repercussions that their parents' divorce has on children. In *Make or Break* (1984) Dominian cited an American study that had just been published, which suggested that the impact on children depended on several factors. A reasonably good outcome was associated with a continuing loving and reliable relationship with the departed parent (normally the father), the presence of a loving and reliable mother, the elimination of conflict, bitterness and bickering between them, and the child's possession of significant social and psychological resources. A bad outcome was related to negative fac-tors in all these areas. A third of the children involved in this study were still unhappy five years after their parents' divorce, while 'the more distressed children tend to show deterioration in their work at school, become emotionally upset, are often depressed, and a proportion develop disturbed behaviour and delinquency'.

In *Sexual Integrity* (1987) Dominian analysed recently available research which had divided a batch of children into four age groups and then examined the impact of the break-up of their parents' marriage on each one. Pre-school children were frightened, unable to understand what was happening, and tended to blame themselves; young school children expressed feelings of sadness, abandonment and rejection, and were desperate to reconcile their parents; older school children realized that divorce was something between their parents, not something they were responsible for, but were angry and lonely, and shocked by their parents' behaviour; and adolescents were often very upset, and gave vent to strong feelings of anger, misery and shame.

In his most recent major work on marriage, *Passionate and Compassionate Love* (1991), Dominian declares that all the available evidence shows that children do not want their parents to split up and that 'many, but not all children suffer as a consequence of divorce'. In one British study divorced families were compared with 'intact' ones, with the effect on boys and girls who had experienced their parents' divorce or separation before they had reached the age of five examined in detail. A number of the boys wet their bed persistently up to the age of fifteen, while a significantly higher percentage than the norm had been convicted of a criminal offence by the age of 21; this was especially true of sexual and violent crimes. It was not only the boys who seemed inadequate. Teachers often rated their mothers as less interested than other mothers in their sons' school progress while health visitors thought that these mothers were generally less competent than the norm, regardless of social class. However, the most disturbing finding of all, in Dominian's opinion, was that there was a distinctly higher incidence of divorce or separation in the boys' and girls' own marriages; and, among the girls, a greater tendency to give birth to children outside marriage.

Dominian also cites different studies of the same evidence, which indicated that whereas parental death seemed to have had very little impact on a child's later educational achievements, children of divorced or separated parents had a significantly reduced chance of obtaining any academic qualifications, and of academic achievement in higher education.

Recent American analysis of divorce 'shows a remarkable agreement' with these British studies that divorce causes children 'widespread short-term behavioural disturbance and long-term social, economic and psychological disadvantage'. Dominian confesses to having been particularly startled by one extensive piece of American research which found that 23 per cent of the fathers in the overall sample had had no contact with their sons or daughters during the entire year, causing the researchers to conclude that 'marital disruption effectively destroys the ongoing relationship between children and the biological parent living outside the home in a majority of families'.

Dominian himself thinks that one of the most devastating consequences of divorce is the number of families that are left with a single parent. The number involved in England and Wales was first estimated in 1971 as 620,000; by 1980 this had risen to 920,000 parents, caring for one and a half million children. Dominian estimates that at present one in seven families is headed by a lone parent, usually a mother.

Every piece of research shows that such families are seriously economically handicapped and that the life of the parent is 'difficult, socially, economically and psychologically', since she 'is under stress, over-tired, harassed and unable to give love, time and attention to the children, work and personal life'. Fatigue and social isolation are frequent. When the parent has to work and look after the children alone, 'the usual outcome is a serious level of tiredness'; when she is not working, 'the level of income may fall seriously to the detriment of both parent and child'.

In 1991 Dominian and his interdisciplinary team at One Plus One, as his Marriage Research Centre had been renamed the previous year, responded to the Government's consultative document on Health by publishing a report called *Marital Breakdown and the Health of the Nation*. In it, they marshalled the stark evidence for the link between broken marriages, poor physical and mental health and above average mortality rates.

The report begins by illustrating the strong link between marital breakdown and premature death, particularly among men; divorced men between the age of 35 and 45, for example, are twice as likely as their married counterparts to die prematurely. Moreover, they are also more prone to ill-health. Such men are more likely than their married counterparts to consult their doctor for almost all categories of illness and especially for infectious and skin diseases, mental disorders, diseases of the respiratory system, and accidents. They are also twice as likely to die from heart disease as married men are, and with their female counterparts, suffer a significantly higher cancer rate.

Dominian and his co-authors proceed to analyse why this is so. They suggest that because marital breakdown normally constitutes a major life crisis for those involved, the stress that is generated compromises the immune function and leads to a wide range of physical and physiological symptoms. In addition, this stress often involves a behavioural response of denial, leading to attempts to ignore the reality of the situation and obliterate the pain it causes, through overeating, overwork, sexual promiscuity and increased smoking or drinking.

The report presents the supporting evidence. Divorced men and women are much more likely than married men and women both to smoke and to drink. Divorced women between the ages of 25 and 34 are almost twice as likely to smoke as their married counterparts, while over half of divorced or separated men exceed the 'sensible maximum level' of alcohol consumption, and one in five between the ages of 25 and 44 drinks more than 51 units a week.

Mental as well as physical health is affected. There is an extremely strong association between marital breakdown and depression, psychiatric morbidity, alcoholism, suicide and parasuicide. For instance, admission rates to mental hospitals are between four and six times greater among the divorced than the married, and they are four times more likely to commit suicide than married men and women.

The report also confirms that children of divorced parents carry a higher risk than children from intact families of experiencing physical and psychological ill-health; that this is so from the time of parental separation, well into adult life; and that children aged less than five at their parents' separation are particularly vulnerable. The co-authors admit that some people will argue that these physical and psychological health problems can be explained by the economic consequences of divorce; but declare that they themselves believe it would be simplistic to assume economics is the only factor that influences such differences in psychological stability and educational performance.

Twenty years earlier, in 1971, when Dominian established his Marriage Research Centre as a registered charity, he sought funds from trusts and companies for its work. The result of one successful appeal was a link with Marks & Spencer. In return for a sizable donation from the company to the Centre, Dominian established a service whereby, between July 1982 and December 1986, he personally saw employees with marital problems who had been referred to him by the firm's medical service. In 1987 he wrote a brief review of the first fifty cases he had counselled. His main conclusion was that marital breakdown 'is probably the single most important hidden vulnerability in contemporary work' with the 'considerable functional disturbances' that result from it making it 'hard to calculate the loss of concentration' involved.

Such was the pioneering nature of the enterprise and the discretion with which its availability was publicized, that most of the 50 people who came to see him were from the company headquarters. Of those 50, only seventeen were men, which confirmed Dominian's strong conviction that men find it far more difficult than women to seek help. However, it was their experience in particular that opened Dominian's eyes to the scale of the problem and gave him further evidence of the extent to which the private agony of divorce goes hand in hand with public cost. He described how he came across 'people who came to work, sat at their desks, and simply stared at their papers unable to concentrate or assemble their thoughts', while 'in other instances the irritability present caused social and emotional chaos all round'. He concluded that 'the alcoholic at his worst can be spotted, removed and treated. The depressed person arising from marital disturbance cannot be identified so easily.'

Over the last decade Dominian has in fact regularly produced and updated statistics which give some idea of the public cost of divorce to the country through social benefits, legal fees, the expense of taking children into care, and additional costs to the NHS and to industry. In *Marriage, Faith and Love* (1981) Dominian suggested that benefits, legal costs, and child care expenses amounted to nearly £600 million annually — and that if the cost of absenteeism from work, doctors' time, prescriptions and hospitalization was added, the sum would rise to one billion pounds. A Marriage Research Centre report in 1984 on *Marital Breakdown and the Future of Marriage* presented detailed data which put the public cost at £879 million — including £425 million for supplementary benefits — independent of the indirect costs to the NHS and industry, and those resulting from divorce-induced crime. Finally, in *Passionate and Compassionate Love* in 1991 Dominian indicates that he thinks a figure of one to two billion pounds is a conservative estimate, and that the public cost of divorce might possibly be as high as three billion pounds.

CHAPTER SEVEN

The Dominian strategy for the prevention of marital breakdown

It is a source of constant amazement to Jack Dominian that despite the enormous emotional and financial cost to the country of the increase in marital breakdown and divorce, virtually the sole official response has been the provision of marriage counselling. Until 1960, as he observed in a recent article, 'the size of divorce was such that it did not impinge severely on society' and so it was understandable that 'the resources available were considered sufficient to help and support the family in difficulties'. Since then, however, the divorce rate has risen by 600 per cent, and yet apart from the changes in the divorce laws, the government, in his opinion, has remained criminally passive. Nor have the Churches or other sections of society been much more responsive.

The charge of inactivity cannot be laid against Dominian himself. He began counselling for the Catholic Marriage Advisory Council in 1958 and 36 years later retains his belief in its potential value; he still counsels couples with marital problems several times a week, both at One Plus One and in his private practice.

However, as early as the mid-1960s, Dominian had become aware that counselling by itself was an inadequate response to a rapidly changing situation. On the one hand he realized that research was urgently needed to provide counsellors with information on when difficulties arose in marriages, how they could be identified, who was particularly vulnerable, and what could be done to help them. On the other hand, his grounding in the behavioural sciences had made him conscious that sociology, psychology, psychiatry and anthropology were transforming the way sexuality, marriage and the family were understood. As a result, by 1966, he was already pressing — in 'Sexuality and psychology' — for 'an institute of sexology and the family'.

Dominian's original vision for this institute was that it would not only provide up-to-date detailed and reliable information on marriage, but would also be a place for 'a continuous dialogue between the behavioural sciences and theology', and so be able to offer 'the best means for implementing the message of the Good News'. However, in the aftermath of *Humanae Vitae* ecclesiastical support was not forthcoming; so Dominian turned instead to the Central Middlesex Hospital where he had been appointed Senior Consultant Psychiatrist in 1968. The governing authorities were receptive to his proposal and in 1971 he founded a Marriage Research Centre in the hospital complex. In the initial publicity Dominian stated that although his personal motivation was Christian, the Centre would be secular in orientation, since he wanted 'to open the services of the unit to the whole of society on a non-denominational basis'.

In the first twenty years of its existence the Centre established its reputation mainly through the quality of three major research studies, *Who Divorces?*, *Marriages in Trouble* and *The Beginning of the Rest of Your Life*. Two books published in 1990, *Wedlocked* by D. Clark and D. Haldane and *The Good Marriage* by H. Garlick and A. Sheppard, while lamenting the general lack of research into marriage, specifically cited the Centre as an exception and praised its distinctive contribution. Indeed *The Good Marriage* referred to the way 'the Marriage Research Centre directed by Dr Jack Dominian has made enormous strides in lifting the lid off what really goes on in marriages in latter-day Britain'. In the same year the Centre became only the second marriage research body to be allocated a government grant, albeit of only £15,000. However, its relaunch in April of that year as One Plus One, in theory a response to the growing number of cohabiting couples, was actually demanded by the precariousness of its financial position, which had severely restricted the Centre's capacity to fulfil its original objectives.

Despite these limitations, Dominian's involvement with One Plus One since 1971 has increased his awareness of the sheer size of the problem of marital breakdown and the scale of its consequences and considerably influenced the direction of his thought. As a result he has gradually evolved a comprehensive multi-pronged plan for the support of marriage and prevention of marital breakdown involving a close working relationship between the government, the Churches, industry and the medical and legal professions. He presented this programme in his most recent major work on marriage, *Passionate and Compassionate Love*, published in 1991, and since then has taken every possible opportunity to communicate it. Indeed, his short article in *The Tablet* of Christmas 1992, a response to the break-up of the marriage of Prince Charles and Princess Diana, argued his case so succinctly and powerfully that a businessman immediately sent One Plus One a cheque for £35,000.

After 36 years' experience as a marriage counsellor, Dominian is very aware when counselling can contribute something of value and when it cannot. From the perspective of preventing breakdown, he believes that its effectiveness depends almost entirely on whether a couple want to remain together, observing in *Make or Break* that if both partners 'wish to do so, effective counselling should ensure this result', while 'when one or both are really determined not to do so, the best counselling in the world is not going to bring about a reconciliation'. It follows that 'the greatest and commonest challenge' in marriage counselling is 'the presence of hesitant uncertainty in one or both partners'.

He himself has become increasingly pragmatic in his attitude to the theory of marriage counselling. He recognizes that no two counsellors work exactly the same way but believes that some general guidelines hold true for all marriage counselling. A therapist needs, if at all possible, to see a couple together rather than individually to avoid identifying with either party and to establish a rapport with them both. Then it is necessary to communicate to them that counselling is concerned with helping them move from a situation of mutual paralysis and judgemental criticism rather than with giving them advice or making moral judgements. The counsellor achieves this by enabling the couple to identify problems, to see what it is that they need from each other but are not receiving, and to understand why that has been so.

Dominian himself uses elements from both the major schools of therapy, the dynamic and the behavioural. His own roots are very much in the former tradition, which is directed towards the resolution of difficulties which have been brought about by an individual's choice of marriage partner. Dynamic counselling works on the basis that partners normally choose each other on a basis of conscious social selection of age, background, education, religion and race, conscious psychological affinity of what they like and dislike about each other, and unconscious emotional collusion, whereby they choose and are chosen because they resemble or are dissimilar to one or both parents. When these unconscious characteristics are positive, a partner tends at first to be idealized so that problems begin when reality intrudes. When they are negative, a partner is often selected because he or she repeats negative parental traits like indifference and domination — which also causes difficulties.

Dominian believes that 'dynamically-based counselling has been immensely productive and rewarding' but he has recently become more sceptical as to its overall effectiveness. Although he recognizes that it is often successful with intellectual well-motivated couples, he thinks that for many clients its non-directional, non-interventionist approach is confusing and difficult to work with. Moreover, 'it may be able to explain the why of a situation, but underestimate the effort that is needed to change. Couples may need to be seen for months, sometimes for years.' More fundamentally, as has already been indicated, he has become increasingly unhappy with the way dynamic counselling emphasizes disturbed childhood experiences as the source of almost all marital problems, and with its tendency to ignore the sociological perspective.

As a result, Dominian has increasingly utilized the insights of behavioural counselling. Behavioural therapy is not concerned with the dynamics of a situation but seeks rather 'to turn punitive, critical aversive behaviour into something positive and mutually rewarding, by increasing the behaviour that pleases and reducing the parts which displease'. Dominian considers 'reciprocity negotiation' and 'communication training' as particularly effective tools in helping bring about such a change in behaviour. Reciprocity negotiation is based on the 'simple concept that effective marriages are much more mutually rewarding than troubled ones'. In such negotiation 'complaints become wishes' — for a change in behaviour — 'wishes become tasks, tasks are imposed reciprocally, and the carrying out of tasks is monitored by the one who requested them'. Dominian thinks that this approach is 'simple, neat and effective when there are no underlying emotional and feeling difficulties, which make it impossible to carry out the tasks'.

Communication training is rooted in the belief that a great many marital problems are the result of the failure of couples to understand each other. It is primarily concerned with transmitting insights as to what constitutes barriers to effective communication. Typical ones include generalizations — 'you never do the housework' or 'he/she never does anything I want' — which need to be translated into specific complaints; and false assumptions about the other's inner world — 'you're only saying that because you're angry about last night' or 'we both think X of Y' — which can cause resentment at one partner's assumption that they know what is going on inside the other.

Dominian's movement away from a narrowly dynamic approach to counselling is one consequence of his involvement with the Marriage Research Centre and, in particular, of the influence of its three major reports. The first of these, *Who Divorces?* (1979), was an attempt to discover some of the social and psychological factors associated with divorce, accompanied by a discussion of its wider consequences and causes. It was followed in 1982 by *Marriages in Trouble*, an explanation of the experience of 29 couples who had sought help for their marital difficulties, examining their attitudes towards the disclosure of personal and marital problems and the significance of gender divisions in the counsellor–client relationship. The third, *The Beginning of the Rest of Your Life* (1988), was a study of 65 young couples three months after their wedding, looking at their experience of everyday married life with its challenges and frustrations and exploring their hopes for the future.

Once this programme had got under way, the Centre began to try to make a reality of the second half of its stated ideal — 'research into practice for prevention'. The next step was educational; the Centre sought to make available to those professionals directly involved in helping the family both its own research and other information garnered from international studies, so that they could respond more accurately to the problems they encountered. A part-time tutor was appointed and by 1980 courses had been given to marriage counsellors, health visitors, social workers and doctors.

This educational initiative was complemented by a counselling and therapy service for couples residing in the Brent and Harrow Area Health Authority. This was developed both as a practical way of thanking the Central Middlesex Hospital for the benefits received from the Centre's location in its grounds and in order to provide a vehicle for experimentation in research.

In the 1980s the Centre began to organize annual conferences and to publish the findings. These conferences were either research-orientated, like 'Domestic Stress and Work Performance — What Problems and Whose Problem?' in 1987, or more general surveys like 'The Survival of Marriage' in 1983 when Ferdinand Mount talked on 'The place of the family in history', Sir Roger Ormrod on 'The role of law in marriage', and Dominian himself on 'Values in marriage — continuity and change'.

The 1990 conference, 'Marriage Revisited', was opened by John

Patten, at that time the Home Office Minister of State, with reports of its deliberations appearing in twelve national newspapers. By then the Centre had not only established a secure reputation for research but had also developed a coherent vision. Its relaunch as One Plus One included a presentation by Dominian of its beliefs, values and aims as they had evolved during the two decades of its existence — in the process clearly revealing the extent of his own influence on the organization.

The basic beliefs of One Plus One were stated to be that men and women aspire to stability and commitment in their intimate relationships, expressed primarily through marriage; that stable intimate relationships promote physical and psychological well-being in adults and in their children; that families where there is security, solidarity, and understanding of each other's needs help their members to contribute effectively as citizens and workers; that children who grow up in such families are likely to be better prepared to form stable relationships themselves; and that since commitment is the cornerstone of family life, it should be a prime concern of society to help adults create and sustain relationships within which the welfare of children can be secured.

Familiar Dominian preferences were also visible in the presentation of One Plus One's values. Its starting point was the reality of everyday life, with any narrow ideological stance strictly avoided. Thus, while it recognized that most people marry and that the family was usually based on marriage, it also acknowledged 'the diversity of domestic patterns in contemporary society', the need for its work to reflect that diversity, and the fact that 'a proportion of all committed relationships' would not survive. Its concern in the latter circumstances was 'with ameliorating the distress which is caused by marital breakdown to spouses and their families'.

According to One Plus One the two principal features of the recent dramatic changes in family life were the contemporary instability of marriage and the changing roles and aspirations of women and, as a consequence, men. Its aims, therefore, were 'to understand these changes and to find out more about the complexities of forming and maintaining intimate committed relationships in contemporary times' and 'to put our original research into practice in order to prevent family breakdown'. This was to be achieved by a policy based on the four pillars of research, counselling and therapy, education and training, and information.

When John Patten opened the 1990 conference he also announced the government's allocation of a grant to the Centre. However, significantly, that grant was tied to an expansion of the Centre's staff. The Centre in the first two decades of its existence had reflected some of Dominian's own strengths and weaknesses. Like Dominian it had a definite and coherent vision and was brimming with ideas and 'ideas people', but just as Dominian has always freely admitted that he is not at his best with details, so the Centre had lacked managers to consolidate its financial position and translate its rhetoric into reality. In those first twenty years it had been funded by charitable trusts and private donations but, as its 1990 business plan acknowledged, existing resources had not 'permitted development of the full potential of the organisation'. Dominian himself had been responsible for fund-raising but this had been erratic and 'at the expense of counselling and management of staff'; as a result, core posts had been kept going through project monies while junior staff who had been trained had not been retained after projects had ended.

Since its relaunch One Plus One seems to have acquired greater financial stability. Its 1991 report *Marital Breakdown and the Health of the Nation* increased its prestige and influence and was an important factor in the quadrupling of its government grant in 1992. Recently it moved into its own premises in central London near Piccadilly. However, even with this new independence, it has only eight full-time employees and is still not always able to fulfil its stated intentions. For example, Dominian, in a letter to *The Times* in February 1990, mentioned the Centre's good fortune in having both research and therapeutic functions and described how 'we are currently channelling the research findings from our recent study on marriages in their early years into a practical training programme for health visitors, GPs and those who have direct access to all young families'. In the publicity for its relaunch as One Plus One it was announced that *Helping Relationships*, 'a training and information package . . . designed to help professionals such as health visitors, social workers, and community psychiatric nurses to improve their intervention skills with people experiencing difficulties in their relationships', was about to be published. Four years later, it has still not appeared and seems to have been shelved altogether.

Although One Plus One has not been able to fulfil all Dominian's original aspirations, there has been a growing recognition of its distinctive contribution to modern sociology. Indeed, in 1991 one of the most eminent of British practitioners, David Morgan, analysed the Centre's three major studies in an article in *The Journal of Social Work Practice* perceptively entitled 'From "the problem of divorce" to "the problem of marriage"; the sociological work of One Plus One — marriage and partnership research; 1971–1991'.

In his analysis Morgan discovered four themes present in all three studies. The first was an increasing understanding of marriage as dynamic rather than static. The second was the growing interplay between the public and private spheres. As marriage had come to be seen in relational rather than institutional terms, with emphasis on the intimate and the personal, so paradoxically, as a consequence of increasing knowledge of marital problems, the intimate and the personal had emerged into the public arena. The third theme was the central importance of gender, understood in terms of social experiences rather than fixed biological differences. And the fourth was the gradual shift from understanding divorce as 'the problem' to seeing marriage itself as problematical. Morgan observed that whereas in *Who Divorces?* the focus had been on divorce as a condition requiring some kind of explanation, in *The Beginning of the Rest of Your Life* it was directly upon marriage; he concluded that the researchers had gradually come to appreciate that an understanding of marriage was required before it was possible to understand divorce, since they were two facets of a single problem.

Morgan proceeded to praise both Dominian himself and the Centre as a whole. He thought that the three studies did have weaknesses — for instance, a relative lack of focus on relationships outside of marriage and the absence of a comparative perspective — but he believed they were a creative contrast to the tendency of most modern sociological studies of domestic life to concentrate on the economic dimension alone:

> it is one of the strengths of the studies that they demonstrate the ways in which everyday concerns, hopes, fears and anxieties may be legitimate areas of sociological enquiry . . . it would seem that the Centre is particularly well placed to explore the complex interplay between the economic and the emotional, and between the public and private faces of modern marriage.

He also appreciated the continuity between research and practice in the Centre's publications, which he put down to Dominian's personal influence, commenting:

it is something of a tribute to the nature of his support that these three studies could both underline his particular commitment to the centrality of marriage while also providing material for a more critical and paradoxical understanding of the marital relationship.

In his February 1990 letter to *The Times*, Dominian had stated that research findings would not only help make marriage preparation more effective but could also 'be a crucial factor in the provision of support for existing marriages by indicating areas of special vulnerability in any couple'. When he had set up the Centre he had specifically intended it to provide a service for the marriage counselling agencies. However, as he declared in *Passionate and Compassionate Love*, 'after being involved for over thirty years in counselling' he had 'come to recognise some unpalatable facts'. Although there were 150,000 divorces each year, even Relate, the largest marriage counselling organization, saw only 50,000 couples annually. 'Many couples do not use counselling. Men on the whole are reluctant to utilise its resources; the majority of couples prefer to sort out their own problems, seeking help from relatives, friends and their doctor.' Furthermore Dominian's experience of couples referred to him personally was that 'some do very well, but many come too late, having exhausted all hope and motivation, and simply desire a certification of incompatibility'. This was 'a view shared by other therapists' and confirmed by Relate's acknowledgment that they only reconciled 15 per cent of the couples they saw.

Dominian does not believe that this means marriage counsellors have little to offer; rather 'we have to think afresh how to use them in a way that is more rewarding'. He himself suggests a change in strategy — moving 'from a programme of counselling at a late stage to prevention, intervening at much earlier stages when the couples still have hope and motivation to persevere with their relationship'. He thinks that there is a need to raise collective awareness and responsibility by alerting people that 'marriage is in the throes of historic changes' and that marital breakdown inflicts immense damage on spouses and children. In addition, 'a great deal more attention has to be paid to marriage as a source of fulfilment of human potential'. All this requires 'above all, a leadership-inspired drive to put marriage on the map'.

Dominian's belief in the value of direct governmental intervention is not a new element in his approach. In 1984, in his address at the Centre's annual conference, he had observed that although the country was accustomed both to dialogue and to partnership between the government and voluntary bodies in relation to many social issues, there was no organized pressure group to lobby an administration in the field of marriage and the family. Such a group would, he said, be able to influence the government to bring about some very necessary changes in policy. It could push, for example, for a clear statement of commitment towards the family in its emerging variety of forms and for the encouragement of voluntary organizations to foster the family's welfare. It could also press for the implementation of the recommendations of a 1979 government document which had proposed a rationalization of administrative arrangements.

That 1979 report had suggested that a central development unit for marital work should take over responsibility for the family from the Home Office, the Department of Health and Social Security and the Department of Education, all of which were dealing with different aspects of policy. This new unit would co-ordinate a policy of both general education about marriage, and preparation and support for it, so that more would be done to help young people in their personal relationships and to enable teachers, doctors, health visitors, probation officers and solicitors to intervene in marriages before difficulties had escalated to crisis point.

Since 1984, while his Marriage Research Centre has continued to press for the integration of health and family policies, Dominian himself has gradually put together a comprehensive and wide ranging programme for the support of marriage. The cornerstone of this plan is education from an early age in personal relationships. He believes, as he declared at that 1984 conference, that 'one of the things that is urgently required is the introduction of suitable courses in all training centres for teachers so that increasingly the education community will become responsible for its own preparation of pupils in human relationships'. This could involve, as he suggested in *The Tablet*, the introduction of a fourth 'R' in school — for relationships.

Dominian believes that in education the inculcation of values is as important as the imparting of knowledge. He thinks that no person should leave school without a basic awareness of the world of feelings, of the nature of modern marriage, and of the psychological difference between men and women. Primary school should instil in a child that the foundation of elementary relationship is always love, which would involve learning about affection, conflict and its resolution, and reconciliation. In secondary schools pupils need to be taught 'the natural history of biological development, the world of feelings and emotions, the difference between the sexes, a historical approach to marriage, and a contemporary appreciation of love and sex within which problems could be discussed'. Youth clubs should offer similar courses, and there and in schools, marriage counsellors should be available to teach and to provide resources for other teachers.

This general education in personal relationships should be complemented by a specific programme of preparation for marriage. Dominian laments the dearth of research in the United Kingdom as to the best method of preparation, but is certain that the Churches have a central role to play and should insist that anyone getting married in a religious ceremony must follow some course of preparation. Ideally each parish should have a team of lay people running a six- to eight-week course once or twice a year for all those couples planning to get married that year.

Dominian himself has created a course — and piloted it in his own parish — of seven sessions lasting two hours each, made up of a talk and a mixture of discussion and pencil-and-paper strategies. The first session begins with an introduction explaining that the course is concerned with human relationships rather than specific religious instruction, and gives the participants the opportunity to get to know each other a little. After this there is the main talk based on the subject of the selection of one's spouse, and on possible danger signals for the future relationship. The second — 'what do we mean by love?' — covers the experience of love received from parents, and the two states of 'loving' and 'falling in love'. The third examines sexuality — the meaning and value of sexual intercourse, the role of birth regulation, and the place of children. During the fourth session there is an analysis of marital difficulties in the first two phases of marriage, and an outline of what counselling involves. The fifth session is theologically oriented — introducing a vision of Christian marriage as a secular reality taken up and made into a divine mystery. The details of the wedding are the focus of the sixth session while the seventh revolves round a liturgy in which the couple renew their commitment to each other.

Dominian believes marriage preparation courses are important but he also recognizes their limitations. In *Marriage, Faith and Love* he declared that 'it used to be thought in the past that such a course was sufficient to see a couple through their married life. Clearly this is not so. Such a course can only anticipate events and their grasp is often intellectual. Facts are seized mentally; there are a number such as buying a house and setting it up, and learning about birth regulation, which are useful to learn in advance, but the day to day living with all its subtle nuances can only be learned in practice later on.' Such a course, if it is to be really useful, must be part of an ongoing programme of support before and, especially, after the wedding — since whatever form the course takes, there is still a need for 'post-graduate education and support for marriage'. Indeed the two central features of Dominian's entire strategy are the provision of as much support as possible in the first phase of a marriage, since those early years are so critical for its survival, and the examination of marriages at regular intervals in all three phases.

Dominian would like to involve voluntary organizations, the health profession, the legal profession, industry, relatives and every other possible resource in this process of support. General practitioners play a particularly important role in his strategy. Millions of people go to doctors with their marital and sexual problems. Sometimes these are communicated indirectly — fatigue, in Dominian's opinion, often being a sign that a wife is doing too much with too little support from her husband; sometimes more directly, especially by wives, who tend to detect problems more quickly than their husbands. Since marital breakdown has such negative consequences for the entire family's physical and mental health, training doctors to diagnose and handle marital problems would be part of good preventive practice. Not only could they play a prime role in helping to persuade couples to go for counselling at a stage when it would be fruitful, but they would also be ideally placed to intervene effectively in two particular problem areas — post-puerperal syndromes and sexual dysfunctions. 'Far too many divorces start with an untreated post-puerperal syndrome' since such syndromes can last for months and sometimes even for years. However, 'a regular check-up after the birth of a baby can ensure that if a syndrome exists, it can be treated with anti-depressants'. Similarly, doctors could diagnose and treat sexual dysfunctions before poor or deteriorating sex becomes a catalyst for marital breakdown.

In addition to their central role in marriage preparation, the Churches also have an important role in other aspects of Dominian's overall strategy. He thinks that each parish should form a marriage and family life committee to provide support for couples at several different levels. Practical help could include setting up mothers and toddlers' groups and youth clubs, and organizing rotas for babysitters — so that young couples would be able to go out alone together one evening a week. Another possible initiative would be an annual day conference on marriage and the family, addressing subjects like changes in the personality and parenting, and offering couples the chance to assess their relationship in such areas as physical and emotional availability, communication and the resolution of conflict. On a more overtly religious level, groups of three or four couples could be encouraged to meet once a month, to reflect on the development of their marriage, and pray together; while sacramental preparation programmes could include elements offering parents the opportunity to examine their marriage.

Dominian believes the Churches also have a prophetic role to play by offering a vision of the ideal marriage: 'the Christian Churches have to reiterate the message about permanency, not as a negative command, but as a realisation of a wonderful gift of love.' A firmly-rooted, evolving, challenging and well-presented theology of marriage could, in his opinion, increase some couples' motivation for staying together in difficult times.

Industry, too, has its place in the Dominian strategy. He thinks it makes financial sense for large companies to provide expert help in the area of marriage since employees' ill-health is such a drain on their resources and marital stress is a leading cause of that ill-health. His work with Marks & Spencer has persuaded him that if a company provided a marriage counselling service which was confidential and close at hand, many working men and women who would not otherwise seek help, would do so. He also thinks that 'where resources permit companies should arrange weekend conferences for their engaged and newly married couples to assist with the work of prevention'. In addition, enlightened employment policies, including flexitime and parental leave, would reduce the strain experienced by partners trying to balance their responsibilities at work and at home.

Since Dominian believes that early intervention is the key to sustaining and improving a relationship in difficulties, much of his overall strategy is geared to making counselling and marriage counsellors more accessible. However, he does not think that 'professional' help is the only way to help relationships in difficulties; parents, relatives and friends can also provide valuable help if 'advice and hurtful criticism are avoided', problems are clarified and 'decisions left to the partners'. In his opinion, relatives will only act in such a non-directive way if their own education has included a study of intimate relationships and given them some knowledge of the challenges in each phase of such relationships. The wheel turns the full circle, returning once more to the foundations of Dominian's strategy — education in personal relationships from the earliest age and the need for reliable, up-to-date research about these relationships.

CHAPTER EIGHT

The Dominian vision of marriage

Jack Dominian believes that God is the source of all love and that human love is the means of exploring divine love. It follows, for him, that marriage 'is the state in which 95 per cent of people will find God in their life', and he cites approvingly the German theologian Walter Kasper's description of it as 'the grammar that God uses to express his love and faithfulness'.

Such a reference is noteworthy because Dominian quotes very sparingly from theologians. One of the few ideas he has borrowed and adapted is the Belgian Dominican Schillebeeckx's understanding of Christian marriage as 'a human reality and saving mystery' — or, as Dominian has presented it, 'a secular reality taken up in the Lord and made into a divine mystery'. This approach has helped Dominian to realize that although marriage is a sacrament, it is fundamentally different from baptism, the eucharist and the other sacraments in that it is rooted not in a fixed concept with an unchanging nature but in an ever changing social entity.

This has significant implications. If the 'divine mystery' of marriage is discovered in the depths of the secular reality, it is necessary to have some understanding of this reality before it is possible to begin to present a vision for Christian marriage. As a result, in the last thirty years Dominian has sought first of all to appreciate the evolving psychological and sociological characteristics of marriage, and only then to combine these with his own scriptural and theological insights. While doing so, as he has observed a striking recent convergence between the secular and Christian ideals of marriage, both seeing it as a community of love — which has led him to the conclusion that Christian marriage has immense evangelizing potential in the contemporary world.

needs. However, one of the major developments in marriage that Dominian has observed in recent years is the way emotional sustaining has gradually acquired equal significance to this material sustaining. He believes this is because men and women, but particularly the latter, want their partner to be in tune with their inner world so that they feel understood in the depths of their being — just as they were by their parents when they were young. Dominian uses the image of a glass of wine as an example of this interplay. The glass is the world of home, work, money and necessary possessions, all needed to sustain the fabric of marriage; the wine is the empathy required to feel each other's inner world and respond accurately to it.

In *Passionate and Compassionate Love* Dominian creates two more 'lists' to illustrate the nature of emotional sustaining in a good marriage. He suggests that there are four characteristics of this type of love: availability, communication, the demonstration of affection, and the resolution of conflict. He then sub-divides one of the four, availability, into three further components. The first is a willingness to spend time together, both in the accomplishment of shared tasks and just alone in each other's company — although he also stresses that the right balance has to be found between being together and being apart. The second, and most important, element of availability is empathy, which he defines as the awareness of one's partner's inner world, and the ability to respond accurately to their need or mood of the moment. The third is presence at the key moments in each other's lives — joyful ones like the birth of a child and more painful times such as the illness and death of a parent. Dominian concludes that this availability is the key to loving since 'its various forms remind the couple of the ever-present embrace of mother or father in childhood, it is the principal feature of exclusivity, and it brings about the daily unity of the couple'. When it is there, 'spouses can bask in the knowledge that they exist for each other, and the strength that gives them makes them available to their children and others'.

Communication is also an essential component of sustaining love. This communication needs to be clear, shared, non-judgemental, appreciative and informative. It requires the ability to listen well and to make sense of what one's partner is saying when he or she is confused — even to the extent of discerning patterns of meaning of which they themselves are unaware. Women, in Dominian's experience, are much better communicators than men, but ideally the different approaches of the sexes to communication — men

more rational, women more intuitive and more aware of feelings —
can fruitfully complement each other.

The third component is the demonstration of affection — outside
the sexual arena. Its recurring expression — through a kiss, a hug
or a touch — is a constant feature of sustaining love since it confirms
that one is loved and cherished. Dominian thinks that this capacity
to demonstrate affection is normally a sign that a couple are in touch
with each other's inner world — and again believes women to be
more capable than men both of giving and receiving it.

The final feature of sustaining love is the ability to resolve conflict. Egalitarian relationships cannot escape some disagreements,
but paradoxically these quarrels can enable the partners to get close
to each other. For a quarrel to be constructive, both partners need
to register the pain the other has experienced or is experiencing and
to seek to understand the causes of his or her vulnerability. When
they do that, not only are they normally able to forgive each other
but they also have an opportunity to heal each other — the second
key component of marital love.

One of the recurring themes in Dominian's writings is that there
are historical forces operating in Western society which impose a
high degree of intimacy in the lives of couples. Another is that a
large percentage of people emerge from their childhood with difficulties in experiencing intimacy. A third — ensuring that the
interaction between these first two need not be disastrous — is that
a good marriage is a most powerful source of healing. Such healing
is closely related to sustaining, since it is in the intimacy of sustaining love that a couple gradually expose their inner world to each
other and reveal the presence of hurt, pain and distress. In addition
to hurts which arise in the course of their marriage, most couples
bring to each other the emotional wounds of the first twenty or more
years of their lives.

These emotional wounds may be genetically determined. Genes
can influence an individual's moods and be responsible for a tendency to depression, elation or anxiety; or they can affect their personality, causing a person to be cold, unemotional, withdrawn or
aggressive. Alternatively, wounds may be acquired in the course of
childhood because of the actions or attitudes of parents or other
important figures. Dominian believes that the more fundamental
wounds are those that are caused by a person's childhood experiences.

These wounds can affect a person's capacity to relate and
therefore can enormously influence the course of their marriage.

Individuals may, for example, grow up with a domineering parent who makes them incapable of taking the initiative or making decisions, or they may arrive at adulthood feeling bad and guilty, considering themselves incapable of loving others or of being worthy of the love of others. Such wounds are often combined with anxiety or lack of confidence and produce men and women who feel unwanted or easily rejected and who find it difficult to express or receive affection. 'Although the extreme forms of these problems affect only a small number of individuals, many people possess some of these features; so that there are few marriages in which aspects of these difficulties do not emerge.'

Dominian believes that in the intimacy of contemporary marriage, these wounds can become part of the shared world of a couple, so that one partner helps towards the healing of the other. When partners' wounds are dissimilar, they can offer to each other the missing components of their personality. The confident husband can reassure his wife about her significance; the loving wife can give her husband the experience of being appreciated. This complementarity ensures healing is achieved in a whole variety of ways, once intimacy has set up the necessary trust and closeness.

However, Dominian is aware that this healing is not automatic and may require a lifetime of openness, careful listening and non-judgemental availability on the part of the other spouse. Sometimes, for example, it will take triggering mechanisms like the birth of the first child or the onset of the menopause before one partner is in a position to further confide their incomplete and wounded self to the other. But if both spouses are patient, and have time for each other, Dominian is optimistic that 'there is no institution which offers so much chance for healing as the intimate relationship of marriage'. Indeed, he believes that 'armed with our modern psychological insight' today 'we face a new era of healing over the fifty years of married life'.

The third characteristic of marital love is that it is a love which encourages the mutual growth of the partners. Whereas a traditional role marriage was largely static and was considered good if both husband and wife carried out their responsibilities as spouses and were faithful and fruitful, today's model of an intimate interpersonal encounter is very different. At its centre are change and personal growth — from immaturity to maturity, dependence to independence, and idealization to reality. Dominian thinks that loving in this context involves a willingness to live with change and to do all one can to assist one's spouse to engage in the same process and realize their potential.

Dominian believes that if a couple are going to encourage each other to grow, the most important prerequisite is an awareness of each other's inner world. Although each person enters into the intimacy of marriage better equipped to understand their own personality, 'appreciating that of our partner is the key to a successful relationship'. Such an appreciation 'implies that we are sensitive to their moods, feeling, values, opinions, priorities and that we respect them' as in the process of change all these will alter slowly and imperceptibly. In addition 'we must not take it for granted that our partner always knows themselves, even though they have experienced themselves infinitely more deeply than we do. Part of mutual growth is acting like a mirror to each other. We can find out who we are by the way we are responded to by another person.'

Dominian distinguishes between general changes — aspects of growth that happen by degrees — and specific processes. General changes may include learning to delay personal gratification until the needs of one's partner and children are met, learning to give in without feeling resentful or humiliated, and growing in tolerance and understanding of the other's point of view. Often this general coping and adapting is 'the hidden basis of love which makes one fond of one's spouse' and leads to increasing respect and appreciation of them.

There are two specific processes, both of which were examined in the analysis of the marital lifecycle, that Dominian makes particular reference to in the context of encouraging growth. He points out that the reduction of idealization is not always a negative experience: 'partners are found to have hidden talents which were not known. Intimacy unfolds many buds.' And he observes that the movement from dependence to independence which is a major challenge in many marriages takes a particular form in those relationships which began in a state of mutual dependence. In such circumstances growth involves both partners gaining confidence and helping each other to take back areas of their lives that they have handed over. In general, 'partnership depends on complementarity. The spouses offer to each other their mutual strengths, but they can also develop additional capacities as they learn from each other.'

Dominian concludes that encouragement to emotional growth ultimately involves helping one's partner grow in their capacity to love. Such love is inextricably bound up with the sustaining and healing elements of marital love since it encompasses a greater ability to communicate, increased sensitivity and awareness of each other's inner world, a growing readiness to accept responsibility, apologize and forgive, and a willingness to encourage and facilitate hidden talents. Ultimately, it extends to the desire and capacity to help one's spouse understand their behaviour and change it to their advantage.

Dominian frequently reiterates that marriage has become an institution for the realization of human potential and that that potential is normally realized by a husband and wife's love for each other involving mutual sustaining, mutual healing and mutual encouragement of each other to grow. But since he believes that it takes a lifetime to get to know another person and to respond accurately to them, he thinks that if a marriage is to fulfil its potential, it needs the framework of permanence.

Dominian recognizes that this concept of marital permanence has strong historical links with the Judaeo-Christian tradition and therefore with an approach that traditionally understood procreation as the main purpose and focus of marriage; and he acknowledges that there is a growing consciousness that people change, relationships die, and individuals need to be free to make new beginnings. However, he firmly believes that the framework of permanence is just as necessary for the intimacy of modern marriage as it was for a children-oriented role marriage, since it is that permanence that makes it possible for partners to meet each other's needs.

This framework of permanence is made up of three essential components — continuity, reliability and predictability. Dominian thinks that a couple need continuity both as parents and as spouses. Children need their parents' continuous presence in the critical years of growth because it enables them to identify with the masculine and feminine parts from which they receive physical care, the stimulus to intellectual and emotional growth and socialization. At the same time an analysis of the inward dynamics of contemporary marriage leads Dominian to assert that in the depths of such a relationship there are needs which demand the continuity of presence of the spouses for each other, quite independent of their role as parents.

If the couple are to sustain each other, continuity is required to give them the chance to learn each other's particular emotional anxieties which need special support. If they are to heal each other, continuity enables them to feel secure enough to expose their

wounds and to allow opportunity for the healing to take place; and
if they are to enable each other to change and grow, continuity gives
time for the unfolding of their own personalities, and the gradual
understanding of the developing self of their partner. Dominian
believes that this continuity is 'a precious truth at the very centre
of permanence' since it avoids 'as much as possible the discarding
of human beings' and the rejection of 'the partner as an object that
can no longer be loved because we no longer make sense of them'.

Reliability is an equally essential component of permanence. Just
as children require the key figures in their lives to be reliable in the
messages they utter, in the responses they give, and in the way
words and actions coincide, so spouses require a similar reliability
from their partner, in their integrity, in the promises they make,
and in their presence at the right time and in the right place. As
with continuity, this reliability needs to be dynamic rather than
static, and to spring from a loving concern which seeks to meet their
spouse's needs. 'Above all reliability is the part of love that will not
fail to answer when called. It means that partners have created a
world for each other which ensures a loving presence no matter what
the difficulties or upheavals may be.'

Continuous and reliable love also requires a core of predictability
and stability. Dominian believes that although this predictability
must never be the enemy of innovation, 'our security, safety and
basic functioning' depend on it, since human beings need to know
approximately what they can expect from those they are close to,
and especially from their spouse. He acknowledges that much of
contemporary Western society is afraid of this predictability, and of
permanent commitment in general, fearing that it could be experienced as a kind of yoke imprisoning a person in a marriage that he
or she feels is burying them alive. However, he himself is convinced
that in order for contemporary marriage to attain its expectations,
this framework is necessary: 'When the possibilities of modern companionship marriage are examined, it is found that sustaining,
healing and growth need a framework of permanence lived as continuity, reliability and predictability. Instead of these characteristics
being seen as destructive of human happiness, they are in fact the
ground on which modern marriage thrives.'

This relationship of married permanence 'has a central experience', sexual intercourse, 'which unites the spouses' and provides
the nurturing that the loving dimensions of sustaining, healing
and growth require. Dominian believes that sex is 'the sustaining

activity which bridges body, mind and feelings and fuses the genital with the affective aspects so that the integral whole plays a permanent part in the understanding of love between the spouses'. If a couple are to sustain each other — in other words, be available, communicate effectively, show affection, and negotiate conflict — they need the constant supply of energy and encouragement that sexual intercourse can offer. Similarly, sex can provide the necessary patience, perseverance and motivation required for partners to heal each other and encourage each other to grow. Responding to one's partner's wounds often in practice involves dealing with the part of them that is irritable, angry, impatient, compulsive, intolerant and generally difficult.

Dominian also believes that a new stage in the evolution of sexual intercourse has been reached and that it is necessary to consider afresh its 'meaning'. As has been indicated, his basic anthropological presupposition is that the prime purpose of sexuality is to form pairing, which he defines as the formation and maintenance of an attachment which then allows for procreation. This bonding is facilitated by sexual attraction and then maintained through sexual intercourse, which has a biological basis. 'The evolution of the human race has made sexual intercourse the means of perpetuating the race' while 'at its very heart is a release from sexual tension fuelled by hormones'.

However, this basic physical dimension is complemented by the personal aspect. Dominian thinks that these days a couple will make love intending to create new life on a specific number of occasions, but that during the rest of their marriage, possibly extending over 50 years, they will seek in their lovemaking 'sexual intercourse's non-procreative intrinsic meaning'.

He himself believes that the personal dimension of sex is its supreme value and that it finds its truly authentic expression in the committed relationship of marriage — because ideally that is when the partners have the greatest meaning for each other. In such circumstances, sexual intercourse is 'a body language of love in which the couple are talking to each other with their bodies' with five key characteristics 'which are not consciously experienced' but which are its 'existential reality'.

The first characteristic is the affirmation of the partners' personal identity. In allowing each other sexual access, a couple are saying to each other 'I recognize you. I want you. I appreciate you. You are the most important person in my life.' Such a gift of a person's body, mind and feelings is a symbol of total availability; the physical becomes the basis for reinforcing the personal. There can be no more powerful affirmation of personhood.

Secondly, sexual intercourse can affirm the partners' sexual identity and significance. A man can be made to feel completely masculine, a woman completely feminine; thus human sexuality is brought to life.

Thirdly, sexual intercourse can act as a reconciling and healing language. Partners will always hurt each other; sex is one of the main ways of healing hurts at a deep level.

The fourth characteristic of sexual intercourse is its ability to convey hope and meaning. The knowledge that at regular intervals another human being wants one, and is prepared to celebrate life with one in the depths of intimacy, can give hope and meaning to people's lives and help them recognize themselves as lovable.

Finally, sexual intercourse can be an act of thanksgiving to and for each other. The partners thank each other for their presence, yesterday, today and tomorrow, and for all that they give each other, not least as a channel of intense pleasure during lovemaking itself. For Dominian the symbol of this aspect is the partners' lying appreciatively in each other's arms in the aftermath of sex.

Dominian is conscious that in emphasizing the existential aspect of intercourse at the expense of the procreative, he is open to the accusation of failing to value the place of children in a marriage. Similarly he is aware that in his vision of marriage there is always a potential conflict between the realization of one's own needs, respect for one's partner's needs, and the care and love required by one's children.

In a symposium in 1986 at the University of Dayton in the USA on 'Marriage in the Catholic Church: A Contemporary Evaluation', Dominian directly addressed this problem. He stated that children were precious and vital to the majority of marriages and that he had no desire to downgrade their importance; however, 'all we have learned from a hundred years of psychology is that the children's stability and happiness depend on the stability and happiness of their parents. There was a man–woman relationship before the children arrived; it is vital that it remain healthy during the period when the children are growing up; after they have left, the husband–wife relationship continues. Thus the husband–wife relationship is the primary one preceding the arrival of children, and succeeding their departure.'

Sexual intercourse in marriage has to be understood in this context. Dominian believes that although on a few occasions it leads to a new life, its significance has come to lie primarily in its key role in maintaining the husband–wife relationship, since at all times it has the capacity to give life to that relationship. When it is absent, so is the existential affirmation it can provide, leaving an immense void.

The following year, in *Sexual Integrity*, Dominian developed his argument. He suggested that the cause of the reduction in the size of families during the last few decades was neither simply the result of the availability of contraception nor a sign of diminishing concern for children; rather, it needed to be evaluated in the context of changes in marriage and in society. He himself believed it was as much a consequence of an increasing awareness of human dignity in various forms as of a 'contraceptive mentality'; and in defence of his thesis he offered four sociologically-rooted reasons.

The first was the rise in the standard of living. Highly desirable objectives like better standards of housing, health, nutrition, clothing and education had been achieved, but a by-product had been the increase in the cost of raising children. That was one reason why more mothers went out to work. The second reason was the growing emancipation and education of women. An educated person frequently desires to realize her potential through work. Dominian believes that the conflict between work and the raising of children has been one of the major causes of tension in Western society in the post-war period. The third cause was people's concern about the size of the world's population in relation to its resources. The sense of shrinking availability of food, whether accurate or not, and increased awareness of the amount of hunger and poverty in the world had also contributed to the diminution in the size of families. The fourth cause presented by Dominian was the growth in the understanding of children's needs. Parents had become more aware that although children could be relatively easily 'serviced' for their physical and intellectual requirements, quality time needed to be given to them if their social and emotional needs were to be met; a reduction in family size increased a parent's availability for each child.

Dominian concluded from this that children remained as precious as ever to their parents and that parental generosity should be judged more by parental attitudes than by the number of children they had. Moreover, the balance that was now being sought between the realization of the spouses' potential as persons and their care of their children had also to be understood in the light of the growing recognition that children's development required the nurturing of the life of the parents. A husband and wife's own love was their offspring's tuition in the meaning of love. 'The child sees in his parents the complementarity of the sexes, learns from them how to be a man or a woman, how to give and receive, relate, fight and be reconciled, be available, make sacrifices, be generous, caring and forgiving; in brief to be a loving person.'

As a consequence, Dominian has strong views about what the relationship between marriage, sexuality and procreation should now be in the developed world. He thinks we need to recognize that an emphasis on the biological and instinctual origins of sexuality is not the most appropriate way to interpret its human dimensions. In other words, sexual intercourse within marriage should not be understood as directed first and foremost towards procreation. Rather its principal role should be seen as the maintenance of the spouses' love both as an end in itself and, since parental love is what a child ultimately depends on for its development, for the sake of the children.

CHAPTER NINE

The Dominian vision for Christian marriage

Jack Dominian believes that God is the source of all love and that human love is the means of exploring divine love. It follows, for him, that marriage 'is the state in which 95 per cent of people will find God in their life', and he cites approvingly the German theologian Walter Kasper's description of it as 'the grammar that God uses to express his love and faithfulness'.

Such a reference is noteworthy because Dominian quotes very sparingly from theologians. One of the few ideas he has borrowed and adapted is the Belgian Dominican Schillebeeckx's understanding of Christian marriage as 'a human reality and saving mystery' — or, as Dominian has presented it, 'a secular reality taken up in the Lord and made into a divine mystery'. This approach has helped Dominian to realize that although marriage is a sacrament, it is fundamentally different from baptism, the eucharist and the other sacraments in that it is rooted not in a fixed concept with an unchanging nature but in an ever changing social entity.

This has significant implications. If the 'divine mystery' of marriage is discovered in the depths of the secular reality, it is necessary to have some understanding of this reality before it is possible to begin to present a vision for Christian marriage. As a result, in the last thirty years Dominian has sought first of all to appreciate the evolving psychological and sociological characteristics of marriage, and only then to combine these with his own scriptural and theological insights. While doing so, he has observed a striking recent convergence between the secular and Christian ideals of marriage, both seeing it as a community of love — which has led him to the conclusion that Christian marriage has immense evangelizing potential in the contemporary world.

Although the divine mystery of Christian marriage has ultimately to be discovered within the framework of the secular reality, Dominian thinks that the task of theology is to offer a vision that will complement and challenge that reality. As has been indicated, Dominian's own theology of sexuality is based on three key texts in the first two chapters of Genesis which reveal that at the heart of God's plan for humanity there is a relationship between a man and woman, in which there is equality, and within which new life can be created. In addition, he believes there to be one other supremely important Old Testament text for a theology of marriage — the prophet Hosea's comparison of the covenant relationship between God and his chosen people to that of a marriage between husband and wife. In that analogy 'for the first time the secular reality of marriage is taken up and made into a divine mystery'.

In the New Testament, the crucial text for a marital theology is the development of Hosea's theme in the fifth chapter of the epistle to the Ephesians. Dominian observes that what is remarkable in this passage is how the writer captures 'the husband–wife unity in and through love as the equivalent of the link between Christ and his Church and plunges marriage into the very depths of divine love'. He also believes that the Pauline view of the body as the temple of the Holy Spirit complements his frequently expressed conviction that sexual intercourse in marriage is 'the recurrent prayer of the couple'. Moreover, 'there is an intrinsic value in which the physical with its pleasure component becomes the basis of the psychological, the existential and in turn the spiritual'.

Dominian asserts that although Jesus never married, he displayed a positive regard for marriage in much of what he said and did. He performed his first miracle at the wedding feast of Cana, interpreted by Dominian as a symbolic act of approval, and he further communicated his respect for the married state by insisting on its permanence and divine origin: 'what God has united, human beings must not divide' (Mark 10:8). Ultimately, Dominian believes that the Old and New Testaments not only testify to the importance of marriage but reveal a richly positive attitude towards it.

Christian Marriage was published in 1967. Dominian had begun to write it when his personal experience as a married man and his clinical experience as a counsellor and psychiatrist were making him aware that there was a conflict between Church teaching on marriage and the reality — both positive and negative — that most people experienced. In *Christian Marriage* he not only examined the scriptural basis of marriage but also traced its history through the centuries, showing in the process that the richness of the biblical vision all but disappeared in the early centuries of Christianity, and was only just beginning to resurface.

This historical survey made him very conscious of the vicissitudes that Christian thinking about marriage passed through in the 400 years that culminated in St Augustine. 'In this long and arduous passage it was impregnated with certain pessimistic, narrow and constricting traits which, while no longer surviving today, have left certain indelible marks on the outlook of Christians.' Some of the reasons for this have already been mentioned, but in *Christian Marriage* Dominian cited three contrasting factors which exerted a negative influence on early Christian deliberations about marriage: the need to establish respect for the state of virginity; the necessity of defending Christianity against heresies like Manicheism which considered the body as evil; and the influence of Greek thought, much of which viewed detachment from passion as the ideal.

This ambivalence about sex and marriage, and sex in marriage, was illustrated by a series of strikingly hostile quotations which Dominian extracted from the writings of the early Church Fathers. Jerome praised marriage solely because it produced virgins. Ambrose considered it a 'galling burden'. Gregory of Nyssa dismissed it as a 'sad tragedy' and viewed it as one of the consequences of original sin. John Chrysostom did not consider it an obstacle to salvation, but thought that since it hindered the greatest possible service to God, it could not be regarded as a perfect state.

Sexual intercourse within marriage provoked a similarly negative reaction. Tertullian assured his wife that none of the improper and voluptuous acts of their married life would be resumed in heaven, for God had not prepared for his own things so frivolous and impure. Jerome declared that 'if we abstain from coitus, we honour our wives; if we do not abstain, well, what is the opposite of honour, but insult?'

Augustine himself wrote a great deal about marriage and had a major influence on the development of its theology. He proposed that there were three blessings or 'goods' in marriage, namely children, the mutual fidelity of the spouses and 'the sacrament', which at that time meant indissolubility.

Fidelity signifies that outside the matrimonial bond there shall be no sexual intercourse; offspring, that children shall be lovingly welcomed, tenderly reared and religiously educated; sacrament, that the bond of wedlock shall never be broken and that neither party, if separated, shall form a union for another, even for the sake of offspring. Such is the law of marriage which gives lustre to the fruitfulness of nature and sets a curb upon shameful incontinence.

These 'goods' became the guiding principle of Christian marriage and, as adapted by the Dominican friar Thomas Aquinas, remained standard Church teaching until the Second Vatican Council.

Augustine also had very definite views on the moral status of sexual intercourse, which was responsible, in his opinion, for transmitting original sin from one generation to the next. He believed that within marriage its inherent sinfulness was removed but only if it was performed for the purpose of procreation; otherwise it remained venially sinful. The Church did not accept all that he postulated but his ideas remained influential. Indeed, Pope Gregory the Great in the sixth century reinterpreted them to propose that whether procreation was the intention or not, the pleasure attached to sexual intercourse was always sinful, and therefore the act itself was too. Dominian believes that this was the lowest point in the history of Christian marriage.

In the Middle Ages there were two significant developments in its theology and practice. The first, in the thirteenth century, was that reformulation by Thomas Aquinas of Augustine's 'goods' into 'primary and secondary ends', the primary ones being the procreation and upbringing of children, the secondary ones, mutual fidelity and the sacrament. In *Christian Marriage* Dominian expressed his dissatisfaction with Aquinas's use of abstract metaphysics to deduce these, and with the way he based his choice of the primary ends on the similarity of the functions of human beings to those of animals.

Around the same time, discussion began as to whether marriage was or was not a sacrament. The debate lasted some five centuries, an official declaration only finally being made at the Council of Trent in 1563. That Council, in response to Luther and Calvin's denial that marriage was a sacrament and conferred grace, proclaimed that

if anyone says that matrimony is not truly and properly one of the seven sacraments of the gospel law instituted by Christ, Our Lord, but was introduced into the Church by men or that it does not confer grace, let him be anathema.

This debate on the sacramental nature of marriage led to two new questions: at what moment were a couple actually married?; and, if it was a sacrament, when was the sacrament conferred upon them? There were two diametrically opposed responses. One, held by the school of Paris, Peter Lombard and Thomas Aquinas, put forward the exchange of mutual consent by the spouses as the starting-point of the marriage and the moment the sacrament was conferred. The other, promoted by Hincmar, Gratian and the canonists of Bologna, declared that it was sexual consummation that was the decisive factor. Eventually, Pope Alexander III decided in favour of the former, because it conformed to the accepted tradition regarding Mary's marriage to Joseph, it was in line with Roman law, and it helped the Church in the campaign it was fighting at the time against clandestine marriages without witnesses. However, he did not reject the Bologna school's view that it was sexual intercourse which rendered the full significance of the indissoluble unity of Christ and the Church to the lifelong bond of the spouses; hence the Church's practice down the centuries of annulling marriages that had not been consummated.

Dominian believes that the decision to come down in favour of verbal consent rather than sexual union as the moment the sacrament was conferred had important long-term consequences. Theological interest moved away from the sexual communion of the spouses towards the initial contractual stage. As a result, there was little study or discussion of the marriage relationship itself, or of the meaning of sexual intercourse within it, and marriage passed primarily into the hands of canon lawyers whose primary concern was to examine what conditions were necessary to fulfil the legal requirements for a wedding. This juridical approach continued to hold sway right up to the twentieth century.

Nor did these centuries see many signs of a more positive general attitude to sexuality. In *Christian Marriage* Dominian cited two memorable examples of this continuing ambivalence. At the beginning of the Middle Ages, certain ascetical writers apparently counselled sexual abstinence for married couples during Advent and Lent, on certain festivals, and also on Thursday in memory of Christ's arrest, on Friday in memory of his death, on Saturday in honour of the Virgin Mary, on Sunday in honour of the resurrection, and on Monday in commemoration of the departed! St Francis de Sales, at the beginning of the seventeenth century, seemed much more positive with his admission that 'marital intercourse is certainly holy, lawful and praiseworthy in itself and profitable to society' but then went on to recommend emulation of an elephant's sexual habits!

> The elephant, not only the largest, but the most intelligent of animals, provides us with an excellent example. It is faithful and tenderly loving to the female of its choice, mating only every third year, and then for no more than five days and so secretly as never to be seen, until on the sixth day, it appears and goes at once to wash its whole body in the river, unwilling to return to the herd, unless thus purified. Such good and modest habits are an example to husband and wife.

The first real sign of a change in the official approach to marriage came nearly three centuries later in 1880, with Pope Leo XIII's encyclical *Arcanum Divinae*, in which the spouses were addressed as individuals with their own personal characteristics and needs. Pope Pius XI's 1930 encyclical *Casti Connubii* took up this theme and developed it by drawing attention to the personal relationship of husband and wife, and by stressing the freedom with which married couples could enjoy sex and its accompanying pleasures.

Casti Connubii inspired the German theologian H. Doms to write *The Meaning of Marriage* (1939) in which he suggested that the use of the terms primary and secondary in speaking of the purposes of marriage should be dropped since 'the union of two persons does not . . . consist in their subservience to a purpose outside of themselves for which they marry, it consists in the constant and vital ordination of husband and wife to each other until they become one'. Doms's book, which Dominian says was a major influence on his own thought, acted as a catalyst for a debate within the Catholic Church as to the meaning of marriage. Discussion continued through the 1940s and 1950s until the Second Vatican Council, which finally abolished the language of primary and secondary ends.

In the Council documents marriage, according to Dominian, was 'placed squarely in the realm of personal love'. The family was described in *Gaudium et Spes* as 'a community of love' whose unique importance lay in its manifestation of 'the Saviour's living presence in the world' through 'the mutual love of the spouses, their generous fruitfulness, their solidarity and faithfulness and the loving way in which all the members of the family work together'. Moreover, the document recognized the strong connection between sexual love and personal love. Personal love was 'uniquely expressed and perfected through the marital act'; such acts 'signify and promote the self-giving by which spouses enrich each other with a joyful and thankful will'.

Dominian's scriptural and historical research made him aware quite how radical — in a literal sense — the Council had been. 'The cycle was completed and the covenant relationship first enunciated fully by the prophets in the Old Testament was re-instated as a major theological character of marriage.' This return to the roots of Christian tradition confirmed Dominian's own instincts and gave him the confidence to construct his own vision for Christian marriage by incorporating insights from the human sciences. Since the publication of *Christian Marriage* in 1967 Dominian has consistently proclaimed and revised and reproclaimed this vision in numerous talks and articles, and in two other major treatises, *Marriage, Faith and Love* in 1981, and *Passionate and Compassionate Love* in 1991.

In 1992 I visited One Plus One and was allowed to take away with me a large collection of unpublished Dominian talks. Five of them were entitled 'Christian marriage', all were different but all followed the same distinctive formula: an introduction; a scriptural and Christian-historical perspective; a sociological and psychological survey of contemporary marriage; an analysis of what married love ideally involves in terms of sustaining, healing and growth, and sexual love; a presentation of the intrinsic meaning of sexual intercourse within marriage; and, finally, an outline of Dominian's own theological vision, and of the practical pastoral support he believes the Church can and should provide to bring this ideal closer to reality.

Dominian's vision of Christian marriage is founded on three basic beliefs: that the sacrament of marriage is concerned with an unfolding relationship covering fifty years or more, rather than with one wedding day; that at the heart of the sacrament is the daily liturgy of married life in the home, the domestic Church, which gives the spouses the chance of a moment to moment encounter with Christ through each other; and that in their daily life as persons united in relationships of love with each other, spouses share in the mystery of the life of the Trinity.

Much of Dominian's recent interest and energy has been directed towards drawing out what the concept of the 'domestic Church' can mean in practice. This description of the family was first used in *Lumen Gentium* — 'the family, so to speak, is the domestic

Church' — and reappeared in *Familiaris Consortio*, Pope John Paul II's apostolic exhortation in response to the 1980 Synod of Bishops on the Family. Dominian thinks 'it is a concept whose importance has not been sufficiently appreciated', since 'within that context the model of Trinitarian love can be lived to the full, and the sacrament unfolds'. He believes that it helps to show how the ordinary experiences of everyday family life can be extraordinary events in which the human meets the divine. 'As we get up every day, wash, dress, have breakfast, go to work, look after the children, return home, cook our meals, eat, drink, talk, and make love to each other, each moment is an opportunity to meet Jesus, in and through each other. Each moment is a challenge to experience God through love.'

Since the members of this domestic Church form a community of love, the foundations of love and faith are laid while a couple and their children are experiencing each other: 'The sacrament offers nothing less than a radical activation of the human into the divine. It is a constant transformation that has no end as the members of the family sustain, heal and grow.'

This sustaining, healing and growth has already been examined from a secular perspective. Dominian believes it to have a definite 'religious' dimension as well. Emotional sustaining, for example, is potentially one of the main meeting-points between human and divine love: couples in a marriage where this kind of sustaining is present can experience something of the unconditional recognition, acceptance and appreciation God alone gives in full.

Similarly, two partners' healing love for each other can be a meeting-point between the human and the divine. At the centre of the Christian faith, as Dominian understands it, is a love which restores wholeness to the human race. He believes that it is because grace is specially present in a marriage to effect an inward transformation that marriage is one of the commonest ways to healing in modern society. He is also aware that such healing takes considerable time, which confirms him in his belief that Christian teaching on the permanence and indissolubility of marriage is a gift to the world, and contrasts strikingly with the destruction involved in the conclusion of so many relationships because difficulties appear insoluble.

Finally, Dominian compares the qualities that a couple need if they are to encourage each other to grow during a lifetime together, with the qualities of the Trinity in which three persons know each other perfectly and respond to each other fully. Moreover, Dominian believes that because this ever-deepening interaction of sustaining, healing and the encouragement of growth gradually unveils the springs of love in a couple, it can help them become aware of the connection between love, mystery and God.

Dominian considers sexual intercourse between husband and wife to be the central and recurrent prayer at the heart of the liturgy of the domestic Church, because it brings the physical and spiritual together and thus truly participates in the Incarnation. He also believes that it strikingly reflects the mystery of the Trinity. That mystery implies a total unity of three persons who at the same time remain completely separate and unique in themselves. Similarly, in sexual intercourse two people are totally united while each retains their completely separate identity.

Dominian himself thinks that marriage is the most important sacrament after baptism and the Eucharist, and indeed that it can be said to include all the essential encounters with Christ that occur in the other sacraments. 'Entry into relationship with Christ, baptism, is reflected in the entry and sustaining of the relationship of the couple. Confirmation is reflected in the constant affirmation that the couple give to each other and their children. The continuous hurt–forgiveness pattern of marriage anticipates the sacrament of reconciliation. The healing effect of the relationship reflects the healing sacrament. The total oneness–separation unity of marriage gives us an insight into the oneness–separation unity with Christ in the Eucharist and Communion.' Finally, Dominian considers that priests and married people are united in their respective sacraments of commitment by the call to relationships of love, since that is the vocation of all human beings.

This stress on relationships of love as being at the centre of the Christian faith is rooted in Dominian's belief that God is the source of all love. He thinks that this belief is a way of approaching God which could and should be a focus for the evangelization of the contemporary world. The natural world of love and sexual attraction is a ready-made interest of that world, and offers the world a chance to become aware of God. Moreover, in his opinion, the convergence of the secular quest for love in marriage with the religious understanding of such love is an opportunity to translate this notion of God as the source of love into practical action, by mobilizing the Church's profound understanding of the inner world of marriage in widespread programmes of marriage preparation, support and enrichment.

The concept of the domestic Church is also important in Dominian's proposed programme of evangelization. He believes the Christian gospel is at heart an odyssey of personal relationships and that the concept of the domestic Church could help the inner world of the family with its emphasis on love to become the basis of that gospel. 'Evangelisation has to start in the home. Everyone has a home and everyone has relationships.' Dominian wants to see 'our century be the beginning of a real spiritual and theological shift whereby the home becomes as powerful a spiritual community as the fellowship of the local Church'.

Dominian refutes criticism that such an emphasis on the domestic Church in a programme of evangelization is too inward-looking and escapist. He believes that working with strangers is, in many ways, an easier option than working with one's family since it does not require the use of those intimate parts of our personalities with which we have difficulties. 'It is the nearest relative who offers the most persistent challenge of love.' Moreover he thinks that once spouses and their children are sensitized to love in depth in their personal relationships, then they become aware of their neighbour with much greater perspicacity.

Ultimately, Dominian believes that the new stress in Western society on love in personal relationships is an unconscious seeking by that society for God, which it no longer expects to find in the institutional Churches. A programme of evangelization which attempts to help people explore God as the source of love in these relationships could, he thinks, lead people back to the Church. However, in Dominian's opinion, that goal is a secondary one. More important to him is whether such a programme increases people's awareness that God is love — the revelation he believes to be at the heart both of the Gospel and of Christian marriage.

CHAPTER TEN

Jack Dominian: A critique[1]

Jack Dominian has become a symbolic figure. Ever since *The Tablet* thrust him into the public eye as one of the champions of its campaign against *Humanae Vitae*, he has been so typecast — a hero for 'progressives', a heretic for 'traditionalists' — that people's reactions to him reveal as much about themselves as they do about Dominian. Two examples suffice. In a recently published book, *The Alliance of Dissent*, a Southwark priest, Fr Michael Clifton, attacks homosexuals, feminists, justice and peace workers, catechetical leaders, charismatics and Medjugorje devotees, but allocates a whole chapter to one person alone — Jack Dominian. In contrast, Adrian Hastings, as was mentioned in Chapter 1 of this book, also points to Jack Dominian, along with Barbara Ward and Kurt Schumacher, as someone who during the 1970s had been a prophet and teacher 'not only for the Church but for the nation'.

The thrust of this book has been much more in agreement with Adrian Hastings's viewpoint than Michael Clifton's. Jack Dominian has made an enormous and very positive contribution to the life of both Church and nation. However, anyone who is as ambitious as Dominian has been in his attempt to bring together the Bible, Tradition, the documents of the Second Vatican Council and the insights of the human sciences in order to produce a vision of sexuality and marriage which is biblical, Christian and human, is taking massive risks and laying himself open to criticism from many directions. Any honest assessment has to recognize the validity of some of these criticisms as well as the extent of Dominian's many achievements and insights.

In January 1980 an article about Jack Dominian in *The Observer* declared 'that there should be a new minister of marriage and it

should be him'. Dominian's greatest single contribution has lain in
the way he — and the Marriage Research Centre that he founded
in 1971 — have helped society and the Churches to come to a better
understanding of marriage as it is lived today.

Dominian's first achievement in this area has been to place marriage in context, by illustrating how it has evolved in the last fifty
years from a 'task-orientated togetherness' to an 'inter-personal
encounter of intimacy', because of powerful social forces such as the
emancipation of women and advances in medical technology.

Secondly, he has created a model of the life-cycle of a modern
marriage which reveals the developmental challenges that need to
be negotiated in each phase, and he has shown how the viability of
such a dynamic unfolding process is dependent on a continuing
realization at a minimum level of its five main dimensions, the
physical, social, emotional, intellectual and spiritual.

Thirdly, Dominian has become one of the greatest living experts
on the causes and consequences of marital breakdown. He has proposed that the main reason for the massive rise in the divorce rate
is the increased desire for, and expectation of, a kind of emotional
intimacy in marriage which draws spouses to a deeper and more
vulnerable layer of their being; and he has illustrated in great detail
the negative repercussions that marital breakdown has for the health
and happiness of the couple themselves, for their children, for their
employers and for society in general.

Dominian has come to believe that divorce is the single most
important social evil in Western society and to realize that effective
as counselling can be in individual cases, it is a totally inadequate
response to the crisis situation that has emerged. His fourth achievement has been to put together a comprehensive and wide-ranging
plan for the support of marriage and the prevention of marital
breakdown which would require a close working relationship between the government, the Churches, industry and the medical and
legal professions; and to press repeatedly for its implementation.

Dominian's fifth achievement has lain in his attempt not just to
support marriages but to enrich them by helping towards a deeper
understanding of what love, and especially love in marriage,
involves in practice. In analysing his own experience as a husband
and a counsellor, he has come to the conclusion that the essential components of marital love are sustaining, healing, and the
encouragement of growth; and that these require the framework of
permanence, in the form of continuity, reliability and predictability,

and the energy that sexual intercourse can infuse into the relationship. Sexual intercourse, in his opinion, has five potential 'meanings' for a committed couple: personal affirmation, sexual affirmation, reconciliation, hope and thanksgiving.

Dominian has also presented his own vision for Christian marriage. He has suggested that the sacrament of marriage is different from the other sacraments in that it is rooted not in a fixed concept but in an ever-changing social entity; and he has brought together the basic Johannine revelation that God is love with the statement in *Gaudium et Spes* that marriage is a covenant of love and life, and sought to make accessible and concrete what such covenant love involves in practice. He has also offered a spirituality for couples based on his belief that marriage presents a husband and wife with the opportunity to meet Christ in each other at every moment of the day.

Dominian's contribution in the area of marital understanding has been immense. He has helped the Church, 'the community of love', to understand the nature of that love, and society in general to appreciate the foundations of, and the need for, stable loving relationships. He has challenged society to respond to the crisis of the rapidly rising divorce rate and offered it suggestions and guidance as to the most effective way to do so; and he has challenged the Church to re-examine its teaching on marital breakdown and remarriage and to alter radically its pastoral strategy in parishes and dioceses. He has shown how the Church has a real opportunity to support marriage both in practical ways and at the deeper level of motivation, and in addition pointed out the evangelizing potential that such a strategy would have.

Despite all these achievements, Dominian's understanding of marriage, and vision for it, have been criticized on several fronts. Among the main criticisms against him are that he has too narrow and introverted a view of marriage, concentrating too much on the relationship between husband and wife at the expense of other relationships inside and outside the family, and ignoring a couple's call to 'fecundity'; and that he writes from a purely Western perspective without acknowledging the different experience of marriage in other cultures.

In 1991 the sociologist David Morgan observed of One Plus One's research that there was a relative lack of focus on relationships beyond marriage, and implied that Dominian himself was partly responsible for this failing. Dominian seemed in a recent interview

to accept the validity of such a criticism; he admitted he had
'emphasized the I-thou relationship because that is what I understand most clearly', adding that 'the community, in other words the
interaction of a number of people, is important to me, but I haven't
developed it a lot in my writings'. Certainly, much of what Dominian writes about the relationship of husband and wife is not exclusive
to them but holds true for friendships and other types of close
relationship.

Not only has Dominian focused rather narrowly on the interaction of husband and wife, but in recent years there has also been
a narrowing of his focus within that relationship itself — the consequence of his increasing emphasis on the importance of the unitive
rather than the procreative dimension of sexual intercourse. In 1967
he wrote in *Christian Marriage* that 'marriage has, from the opening
chapters of Genesis a twofold aim, sexual complementarity and procreation, and this in fact forms an indivisible unity for the overwhelming majority of married couples. Whenever one loses sight of
this central truth in deliberation or in practice, the perfect
balance of the Creator's design is also in danger of becoming
blurred.' Over the last 25 years, Dominian himself has seemed
gradually to lose sight of that 'central truth' and of the second half
of the ideal expressed in *Gaudium et Spes* of responsible and generous
parenthood. The reasons for this probably include the polarization
of debate after *Humanae Vitae*, and — since Dominian has always
been influenced by his personal experience of married life — the
fact that his and Edith's fourth and final daughter was born in 1964.
Certainly, in his later books he seems to have forgotten how large
a part of sexual desire can be the desire for a child.

In addition, Dominian's stress on the unitive element in sexual
intercourse at the expense of the procreative has been criticized not
only because it is one of the bases of his belief in the acceptability
of the use of artificial contraception, but also because such an
approach could be used to justify homosexual genital activity.
Dominian himself prefers to remain largely silent about what seems
a logical extension of his argumentation, but appears implicitly to
accept the validity of its use in a defence of stable loving homosexual
relationships.

Whatever one's views on these issues, Dominian, in my opinion,
is open to the fundamental criticism that he fails to appreciate that
'fecundity' in the broadest sense is an essential element in all loving.
His stress on the immanence of God has caused self-realization to

replace fruitfulness at the centre of his vision for married couples.

This accusation leads into another significant criticism — that Dominian seems to assume that 'the interpersonal encounter of intimacy' that has become the expectation of marriages in the First World is the purpose of, or ideally should be the purpose of, marriages everywhere else in the world. Such an attitude is implicit in his attack on *Gaudium et Spes* for its failure to be more specific about what married love involves in practice; and in his description of the 'global transformation' in outlook which he thinks has changed the nature and expectations of contemporary marriage. In practice 'his field of vision is very limited', as a contemplative nun who has lived for many years in the Third World has observed. She believes that in Africa, for example, sexuality and marriage always have a social aspect and that in that continent Dominian's separation of love and procreation would be an artificial one: 'the African vision of sexuality and marriage embraces so much more than the life and love of the couple and gives it a deeper meaning.'

Dominian has also been validly criticized for the extent to which he presents sexual intercourse as the fundamental centre of every marriage. Barbara Phanjoo, a respected and experienced CMAC counsellor in Edinburgh, is one person who believes that his presentation of its role in marriage is idealized, far removed from what the majority of couples experience. Indeed, she thinks that this is symptomatic of a general tendency in Dominian's writings to present so idealized a vision of marriage that it fails to resonate with the experience of many spouses. In her opinion, partners are almost as likely to clash because of financial difficulties — largely ignored by Dominian — as they are because of sexual ones.

These criticisms cannot be ignored. Yet Dominian's exclusive concentration on the relationship of husband and wife — at the expense of the potentially complementary understanding of marriage as a contract — and his supremely positive approach to sexual love can be defended as an understandable reaction against hundreds of years of Christian tradition. For much of that time, the Church has displayed a persistent ambivalence about the relationship between husband and wife, and the role of sexuality in marriage. Indeed, it has appeared to prefer to focus attention on almost any other aspect of family life, such as the responsibilities of parents for their children, and any other form of commitment, in particular those of priesthood and religious life. It is a characteristic of Dominian's approach that he sometimes makes sure his voice is heard by taking up a relatively extreme stance.

However, there are other more damaging criticisms which are less easy to rebut. They fall into four areas: of methodology; of theology; of anthropology; and of manner and style.

One of the most striking features of Dominian's overall vision of sexuality and marriage is the coherence of his synthesis of the psychological, the sociological, and the theological whereby it forms an organic whole. Dominian's solid psychological training ensures his anthropology, although eclectic, is soundly rooted. However, he does not have the same professional background in theology. As a consequence, in his methodology he has no real option but to follow his instinct — which is intuitive and inductive — and to make the human person, rather than revelation, his starting-point. In doing so, he enters a debate which has been one of the major tensions within the Catholic Church since the Second Vatican Council, firmly on one side. This debate concerns the correct way to 'do theology'.

In this debate, the argument revolves around two main methods of 'doing theology' — the deductive and the inductive. Traditional proponents of the 'deductive' method believe that theology and anthropology are not identical and therefore that it is not possible to read God's will from human experience. This approach has, however, been modified in recent years by some Catholic theologians, including Hans Urs von Balthasar, Walter Kasper and Carlo Maria Martini, who have sought to escape from the narrow deductive logic of scholasticism and to work with revelation in a more dynamic way in order to throw light on our human experience.

The inductive approach — originally associated in particular with the Swiss theologian Paul Tillich and the Canadian philosopher Bernard Lonergan — attempts, instead, to work upwards from human experience towards transcendence, seeking areas where that experience resonates with revelation. The Second Vatican Council and in particular *Gaudium et Spes* — as Karl Rahner and Yves Congar indicated — acknowledged the importance of human experience as a source of doctrine and seemed to encourage a dialogue between theology and the critical secular disciplines. The danger of such a methodology, however, is that human experience can be projected onto God so that God ultimately becomes a human concept. Since the Council, the Magisterium has retreated from its initial openness to the inductive approach, and to view its proponents with increasing suspicion. Pope John Paul II's recent encyclical *Veritatis Splendor* can be better understood in the light of this debate.

Since the Council, Jack Dominian has been one of those human scientists who have responded to the challenge presented by *Gaudium et Spes*. He has gradually developed a theology of sexuality and marriage that is based on his own intuition and experience — and which he has sought to 'match' with divine revelation. The response to this has not always been favourable. The Dominican Brian Davies, among others, has criticized Dominian's approach as not susceptible to rigorous logical demonstration but proceeding from proposition to judgement using general practice and personal experience as a guide. Yet, at his best, Dominian has successfully negotiated a *via media*, showing how revelation can affirm what is already present and helping people to understand how sexuality is at the very root of human existence and how love in the Godhead and love in the roots of human nature are inextricably entwined.

Although Dominian has been criticized for this inductive approach, his real problem has lain less in his methodology, which, in my opinion, is a valid one, as in his failure to sustain it. For all his self-confidence and conviction, he is a psychiatrist rather than a theologian. In practice, in his synthesis of the psychological, sociological and theological, he seems to have assumed that the theological is identical with the sum of the psychological and the sociological, and to have proceeded to select those passages from the Scriptures and Vatican II documents and those elements from Tradition that 'fit' his anthropology. In addition, because he is a psychiatrist first and foremost, his starting-point has been a psychological understanding of the human person, and he has not seemed willing to engage in dialogue with the biblical, dogmatic and spiritual insights into the nature of that person and of God, or to accept that theology and spirituality can be valuable aids in grappling with what it means to be human. Similarly with his rejection of the value of philosophy — many who would agree with him that love has to be at the centre of Christian theology would also assert that the task of offering a rational justification for the credibility of love in that context is not one that can be sidestepped entirely.

It is in this area of theology that Dominian's limitations are most apparent. Because his vision of God is dictated by his anthropology rather than by revelation, this vision is of an entirely immanent

God, possible, as one of his former colleagues at One Plus One
pointed out, to caricature as a 'psychological big thing called unconditional love'. Certainly, that is the impression given by a passage
in *From Cosmos to Love* when Dominian asserts that 'the greater
humanity's understanding of what loving means, the nearer it is to
the mystery it calls God'. Such an approach does not seem to allow
for a transcendent yet personal reality outside human beings whose
existence colours and qualifies all human relationships; indeed, as
he stated in a recent interview, Dominian views himself as 'a
tremendous protagonist against the idea of a vertical relationship
with God', since he believes 'you have got to go through your
neighbour to God'.

Inevitably, a belief in such an immanent God affects Dominian's
understanding of Jesus. He fails to recognize that Jesus is a
paradigm not so much of our humanity as of God's assumption of
our humanity; while, from a theological perspective, Dominian's
stress on sexuality as the cornerstone of our humanity requires a
more Christological framework, a balancing emphasis on Jesus
Christ as the cornerstone of God's humanity.

Dominian's failure to develop a theology of the Holy Spirit,
however, is the most unexpected and damaging of his theological
limitations: unexpected because his stress on experience and on an
immanent God would in many ways lend itself to such a theology;
and damaging because so much recent theology has been based on
a 'recovery' of a theology of the Spirit. Although this renewed
pneumatology stresses just those elements — person, love and relationship and people's personal experience of the living God — that
are at the heart of Dominian's own approach, he seems to be blind
to its potential. One consequence of this is that he fails to distinguish
between human sensual created love — *erōs* — which does not exist
in God; and the unconditional love of *agapē* — which is the real way
human love reflects the divine. Another is that despite his
frequent Trinitarian references, Dominian's Trinity in practice
resembles a 'Binity'.

The other main theological criticisms made of Dominian's vision
also have their foundation in the way his anthropology provides the
parameters for his theology, and his consequent failure to balance
God's immanence with His transcendence. Dominian has been
criticized, for example, for failing fully to respect the Scriptures —
and for seeking 'proof texts' to illustrate his anthropological presup-
positions in a manner one critic has described as 'uncatholic,

unscholarly and unconvincing'. Certainly, he can validly be accused
of creating his own Canon within a Canon — comprising Genesis,
Hosea, the Song of Songs, the Johannine letters and gospel, and the
Pauline passages about love — since he makes very few, if any,
scriptural references outside these books.

Similarly, his understanding of the Fall as 'human awareness of
incompleteness' and of sin as 'a failure to capture the fulness of
humanity' can be challenged. Are we always wounded but never
sinners? The psychiatrist in him seems to have difficulties with
purely theological concepts.

Dominian's introspection and intuition combine to make him an
original thinker, but although they are responsible for his insights,
they are also the cause of some of his 'blind spots'. This is particularly true of his attitude to prayer. He acknowledges that he
himself finds it difficult to pray in the 'traditional' way and it is
true, as he says, that a monastic spirituality rather than one which
recognizes the reality and priorities of daily life has often been
recommended for the laity. However that does not really justify
Dominian's reinterpretation of prayer as 'the understanding and
achievement of love in human relations'; or his conclusion that
for all married couples the main way of praying is by loving each
other, since prayer is really just 'the human moments preoccupied with achieving love', and 'every moment' of a couple's 'mutual
awareness'.

Moreover, Dominian's failure to retain a balance between
transcendence and immanence in God ultimately strikes at the root
of his own vision of a God of love. There is something very frighten-
ing about a God who is only to be encountered in human beings'
love for each other; such a God has moved beyond the reach of those
people who, through no fault of their own, are so emotionally
damaged that they are unable to love.

These theological omissions and distortions, and their consequences, are the most fundamental of all the criticisms that Dominian faces. Indeed, they might seem to invalidate his entire corpus.
Yet there are mitigating factors. One is that the flaws in Dominian's
theology are partly rooted in two of his most impressive virtues: his
strong desire to develop a Christian humanism, and his deep
awareness of the Christian imperative to evangelize. Dominian
believes a pluralistic society will only accept Christian teaching if
it is presented as reflecting human authenticity. This would appear
to have been a further factor in causing him to ignore God's

transcendence; a recognition of God's transcendence brings with it the 'faith' dimension of Christian morality, and makes it much more difficult to present such morality as identical with human integrity.

In addition, it has to be remembered that when Dominian began to develop his vision, he was a relatively early Catholic proponent of a relatively new Catholic way of 'doing theology'. Nor is it as if his theology is inconsistent and error-strewn; rather, it illustrates the difficulties of trying to create a theology out of a psychology. Indeed, Roland Walls believes that the basic problem with Dominian's theology is that it is out of alignment, 'riding on the sleepers rather than the rails', even if it would now require a massive readjustment to bring Dominian into constructive dialogue with von Balthasar, John Zizioulas and other relational theologians.

Nevertheless, the fact that Dominian has not read these theologians, nor shown any interest in them, suggests that on balance he might have been wiser to have adopted a different approach from the one he chose. It would perhaps have been more prudent either to have presented his synthesis of psychology and sociology and the insights they offer and left the further synthesis with theology to someone more theologically competent; or, alternatively, to have offered his vision more as a personal subjective and devotional 'response' than as the theological 'solution'. As it is, his consistent failure in recent years to engage in dialogue with other theologians, and to show that he is still listening respectfully to the official Magisterium of his Church, goes some way to explain his inadequate understanding of God.

However, it is ironic — and indicative of the complexity of the task Dominian has set himself — that just as his theology is criticized for being dependent on his anthropology, so his anthropology is criticized because of the influence of his theology. Dominian himself has stated that he believes 'a genuinely Christian anthropology has to be optimistic'. Certainly, the main anthropological criticisms he faces are the consequences of this optimism, since several of his critics think his belief in a God who is love causes him to underplay human limitations and to omit the whole realm of psychopathology.

The psychiatrist Dr Seymour Spencer questions Dominian's overall interpretation of the attachment theory: can babies really be said to fall in love with their mothers? Is early infantile bonding as

exclusive as Dominian suggests? Why does he omit Winnicott's
stress on the egocentric element in such bonding? Similarly, the
ethicist and philosopher Roger Burggraeve is critical of Dominian's
failure to acknowledge the ambivalence of desire in the early stages
of a loving relationship, while other psychiatrists lament Dominian's
omission of Adler's insights into power and aggression.

The moral philosopher Ian Thompson summarizes the main
thrust of these criticisms by declaring that Dominian seems to ignore
the 'conflictual ambivalence' of human sexuality. The consequence,
in Thompson's opinion, is that Dominian 'deals with our human
experience in a way that is only half the story; it is like "the sound
of one hand clapping". It is a landscape of only two dimensions,
length and breadth but no height or depth . . . the emphasis on the
positive as the norm means that his account of the pathology of our
lives sounds superficial and unreal.'

Again, these are important criticisms and are difficult to reject
totally. Dominian's psychology explains his muted approach to sin;
his theology causes him to play down the darker side of human
nature; both combine to focus on the capacity for love in each individual. The result is an optimistic anthropology which fails fully to
reflect reality. Yet, a similar defence to the one presented for his
theology is valid for this anthropology. Dominian is attempting something relatively new, seeking to integrate different disciplines. His
vision is a vision — a conscious presentation of an ideal; it has an
inner dynamism; the value of the whole is greater than the sum
of the parts, and, flawed as the overall outcome is, it still offers new
insights.

In addition, it must always be remembered that Dominian's
primary objective is a pastoral one — the practical need 'to keep
people afloat' and help them. His anthropology reflects that; he
knows from personal experience the advantages of an optimistic
outlook in counselling — because of the effect of positive trans-
ference. Similarly, as one brought up on pre-Vatican II Catholicism
with its stress on sin and the dangers of sexuality, and with his
knowledge of the history of Christian marriage, he is very conscious
that the other pessimistic 'story' has been told for so long. He
strongly believes it is time that Christian lips are heard proclaiming
the goodness and beauty of sexuality and marriage.

The fourth major area of criticism concerns Dominian's manner
and style. Jack Dominian is in no doubt that he has had an important, even a prophetic, role to play in the life of the Church, and

to a lesser extent the nation, during the last thirty years. Nor has he ever had any doubts about the importance of the message that he has been proclaiming in that time. In *The Tablet* of 2 May 1992 he reviewed the book *Catholics and Sex*, a companion to the television programme of the same name. The review is vintage Dominian, managing in a short space to tear the book to shreds and to inform the authors that they should have been addressing the important issues, the ones he himself has been examining during the previous decades!

> Christianity as a whole and the Roman Catholic Church in particular have a serious problem with human sexuality . . . I have found almost universal agreement that a new approach is urgently needed for the sake of evangelization . . . What we have seen in our age is a change in the understanding of sex which is no longer regarded as primarily a biological function, but as an expression of a loving interpersonal relationship . . . It is a concern with this fundamental new approach that I was looking for in this book. Unfortunately I found its price excessive, its contents filled with familiar criticism, couched in language approaching the vulgar, its understanding of Christianity crude and mistaken, its attempt to explore the way forward a dead end . . . The challenge to the Church is to move from a biological philosophy of sex, based on natural law, to a personalist understanding of sexual intercourse as a body language for transmitting love . . . the book is right in its criticism of some traditional Christian teaching. It is right about sex being a minefield and the authors would have done better to be aware that those who are trying to work out a new sexual morality have to be careful not to blow themselves to pieces in the process. Kate Saunders and Peter Stanford seem to believe that a mere reversal of present teaching is all that is needed. Alas that is naive as is their whole book. What is required is a penetrating examination of how sexuality is related to love in an interpersonal journey that lasts some fifty years or more.

The familiar Dominian characteristics are evident: the broad sweep; the diagnosis of the problem; the confident dissection of mistaken solutions; the decisive presentation of the correct way forward. Cardinal Hume in an interview specifically cited the final sentence of that review as an example of Dominian at his most impressive, clearly articulating what the Cardinal agreed was one of the most important challenges facing the contemporary Church — the need to marry love and sexuality.

But, paradoxically, that review also illustrated exactly why Dominian has been criticized for his manner and style. Much of what he attacks in Stanford and Saunders — accurately — are criticisms that have been made of Dominian himself: a mistaken understanding of Christianity, the naïve desire simply to reverse present teaching, the repetition of familiar criticism. The review highlighted another frequent criticism made against him — his tendency to make simplistic generalizations and to caricature the position of others. As Cardinal Hume pondered in the same interview, was sex in the past, for instance, 'ever really regarded as primarily a biological function'?

Criticisms of 'manner' lead into criticisms of style. As a reviewer of one of his books declared, his writing 'seems to lack vitality; there are virtually no examples taken from the world of everyday experience . . . Dominian speaks in generalities: adolescents, the people we love, spouses and teachers. No concrete person, no specific story emerges from the text to capture our imagination; further, the observations and analyses seem old; no new ground is broken here. No new perceptions glance off the rock to enlighten.'

Again, I believe that these criticisms are for the most part valid. Dominian is not always accurate in the way he presents others' viewpoints. His prose does not always inspire. He tends to repeat himself. He can sound and appear self-important; indeed, as one bishop observed, his everyday manner still resembles that of the Senior Consultant he once was. Yet, as so often, these are the disvalues of Dominian's virtues. He communicates simply, effectively, clearly and with great authority. He seems to have consciously chosen not to write anecdotally and imaginatively —but rather to have opted for the 'scientific' route, seeking to act as a bridge between Church and world, religion and science.

Above all, if Dominian has sometimes sounded self-important it is because he genuinely believes in the importance of his message. He sees himself as a prophet with a prophet's mission and like most prophets he views his task as to proclaim this message, reserving his listening skills for his clients.

Dominian's outstanding achievement has lain in his fulfilment of his vocation to help and challenge society and the Churches to come to a better understanding of marriage as it is lived today. However, the prophetic aspect of that vocation has also overflowed into other areas.

For over 25 years, Dominian has been one of the prophets of a lay movement which began to challenge traditional clerical authority within the Church even before the promulgation of *Humanae Vitae*, and has continued to do so ever since. Studying the documents of the Second Vatican Council just after it ended, Dominian realized that there were certain passages in these documents which ensured that there could never again be a clear distinction between the 'teaching church' and the 'learning church'. These passages in *Lumen Gentium* and *Gaudium et Spes* were like 'unexploded bombs' since they declared, for example, that the laity shared in the prophetic activity of the Church; that the Church required 'special help' from social scientists; and that the 'individual layman by reason of the knowledge, competence or outstanding ability he may enjoy' was permitted and even obliged 'to express his opinion in things which concern the good of the Church'.

The Church had stated that experience mattered, that it had much to learn from the human sciences, and that there was such a thing as loyal dissent. Dominian, through his repeated communication of these passages, and by basing his own approach and strategy on them, has left uncovered something that is fundamental to the nature and future of the Church.

Dominian has also, despite the defects and omissions in his dogmatic theology, been a prophet and a pioneer of a new way of doing theology, encouraged and validated by *Gaudium et Spes*. As early as 1967 he was challenging moral theology to come to terms with the historicity of the human person, writing in *Christian Marriage* of the need to accept the limitations of each individual and to exercise 'enormous patience and tolerance for a simple step forward'. He continued by pointing out that 'what one person may achieve in a year may be for another a decade's hard sweat and for a third a lifetime's unattainable effort'. If Christianity was to be criticized it was 'for giving the impression at times that nothing but perfection is acceptable and that anyone unable to achieve it had better seek a refuge elsewhere'.

Dominian's rejection of a static view of the human person, and his recognition of the importance of the stages of growth, and of the need to take account of where a person has reached on a graph of interrelationality, has helped to challenge both ethicists and pastors to move towards an understanding of an ethics of growth.

In addition, Dominian has sought through his principle of sexual integrity to provide an alternative anthropological foundation for aspects of the Church's teaching on sexuality and marriage. He realized that if the Church was going to address human beings and retain credibility, it needed to integrate the self-understanding offered by psychology into its overall approach — since all that is known about relationships springs from human experience. As a consequence, in his adaptation of attachment theory he has sought to show how sex without affectivity can possess neither vitality nor authenticity, since from the earliest days of life human interaction occurs where affective feelings are present.

Furthermore, Dominian has created a coherent vision of sexuality which can claim to be both Christian and human. Such an inductive approach challenges the largely deductive methodology of the official Magisterium — especially if it is accepted that a knowledge of psychology is one of the ways we come to an understanding of Natural Law. Moreover, his stress on the unitive rather than the procreative element in sexual intercourse implicitly offers an alternative way of assessing the morality of those two issues which will continue to confront the Church — contraception and homosexuality.

The third area in which Dominian can be considered a prophet is a very personal one. It is possible, I believe, to present him as a symbol and a prophet of the lay vocation itself. He has remained faithful to a pilgrimage of faith that began in Athens in the 1930s, and which evolved in the 1960s into a vocation within a vocation which he still pursues today. Cardinal Basil Hume, among others, has recognized and admired Dominian's persistent dedication to this calling to help 'people to understand the place of sexuality in their own love life and the relationship of sexuality to loving'.

Sometimes, this mission has required Dominian to plough a lonely furrow but, supported by Edith, he has given of himself unstintingly for over three decades; and he continues and will continue to do so. In September 1993 I asked for one final interview for this book. Edith insisted that I stay the night. We talked and dined and talked again, and then just as we were going to bed, I asked when Jack was going to retire. Edith answered for him: 'Jack will never retire, provided there are patients he can still help. He views it as a moral obligation.'

Note

1 I am grateful to Cardinal Basil Hume, Br Roland Walls, Professor Roger Burggraeve, Professor Ian Thompson, Mrs Barbara Phanjoo and Dr Seymour
Spencer for making time to discuss their views of Jack Dominian with me during
the preparatory work for this chapter.

Bibliography

Books by Jack Dominian

Psychiatry and the Christian (London: Burns and Oates, 1962).
Christian Marriage: The Challenge of Change (London: Darton, Longman and Todd, 1967).
Marital Breakdown (London: Penguin, 1968).
The Church and The Sexual Revolution (London: DLT, 1974).
Cycles of Affirmation (London: DLT, 1975).
Authority: A Christian Interpretation of the Psychological Evolution of Authority (London: DLT, 1976).
Depression (London: Collins, 1976; 2nd edn 1990).
Proposals for a New Sexual Ethic (London: DLT, 1977).
Marital Pathology (London: DLT, 1980).
Marriage, Faith and Love (London: DLT, 1981).
The Growth of Love and Sex (London: DLT, 1982).
Make or Break: An Introduction to Marriage Counselling (London: SPCK, 1984).
The Capacity to Love (London: DLT, 1985).
An Introduction to Marital Problems (London: Fount, 1986).
Sexual Integrity: The Answer to AIDS (London: DLT, 1987).
Human Relationships: A Short Introduction (London: St Paul's, 1989).
Passionate and Compassionate Love (London: DLT, 1991).

Joint-Author Works

With A. R. Peacocke, *From Cosmos to Love* (London: DLT, 1979).
With H. Montefiore, *God, Sex, and Love* (London: SCM, 1989).
With E. Flood, *The Everyday God* (London: Geoffrey Chapman, 1993).

Chapters in Multi-Author Works

'The nature of marriage' in J. Marshall (ed.), *The Future of Christian Marriage* (London: Geoffrey Chapman, 1969).

'Personal maturity' in G. Meagher (ed.), *Priest: Person and Ministry* (London: Gill and Macmillan, 1970).

'Marriage and the family' in J. Cumming (ed.), *The Church Now: Catholic Church in Britain and Ireland* (Dublin: Gill and Macmillan, 1980).

'Christian marriage' in W. Roberts (ed.), *Commitment to Partnership* (New York: Paulist Press, 1989).

'Sexual love, secular reality — divine mystery' and 'Christian marriage' in L. Swords (ed.), *Selected Homilies for Marriage and Penance* (Dublin: Columba Press, 1989).

'The consequences of marital breakdown' in W. P. Roberts (ed.) *Divorce and Remarriage* (London: Sheed and Ward, 1990).

'What is human development for priests?' in *Priestly Development in a Changing World* (Dublin: Dominican Publications, 1991).

Others

'Marital breakdown and the future of marriage', *Long Range Planning* vol. 17 no. 2 (Oxford: Pergamon Press, 1984).

Foreword to B. Fletcher, *Clergy Under Stress* (London: Mowbray, 1990).

'Divorce' in *The New Dictionary of Catholic Social Thought* (Collegeville, MN: The Liturgical Press, August 1990).

'The pastoral experience' in *The Companion Encyclopaedia of Theology* (London: Routledge, 1994).

Booklets

Marriage: Making or Breaking (London: Family Doctor Publications, 1987).

Marriage and Sexuality (All Church Series, Ealing Abbey, 1993).

Articles

'Family limitation: a Catholic doctor's view', *Blackfriars* (May 1961).

'Love in Christian marriage', *Catholic Herald* (24 August 1962).

'Sexuality and psychology', *The Month* (September 1966).

'Vatican II and marriage', *The Clergy Review* (January 1967).

'To serve the poor: a prospectus for an Institute of the Family', *Theology* (October 1967).

'The Christian response to marital breakdown', *Ampleforth Journal* (Spring 1968).

'Psychoanalysis and the Christian life', *New Blackfriars* (September 1968).

'Forgiveness and personality', *Theology* (November 1968).

'The available priesthood: the sacred ministry', *Theology* (April 1969).

'The psychological roots of authority', *New Blackfriars* (July 1969).

'Human and divine love', *New Blackfriars* (September 1970).

'Pornography', *The Clergy Review* (October 1970).

'What is sensitivity?', *The Way* (April 1971).

'The guilty conscience', *The Way* (October 1971).

'Authority and paternalism', *The Way* (July 1972).

'Emotional maturity and the priesthood', *The Clergy Review* (July 1972).

'Helping the homosexual', *St Anthony Messenger* (June 1973).

'The changing nature of marriage and marital breakdown', *The Clergy Review* (June 1973).

'Birth control and married love', *The Month* (June 1973).

'The function of prayer at a time of crisis' *The Month* (June 1975).

'The relationship between Christ and Mary', *The Way Supplement* (Summer 1975).

'The wholeness–holiness dimension of priesthood', *The Clergy Review* (June 1976).

'Psychological evaluation of the Pentecostal movement', *Expository Times* (July 1976).

'The sexual revolution: breakthrough or déjà vu?', *The Clergy Review* (January 1978).

'Grief', *The Furrow* (July 1978).

'Bereavement', *The Franciscan* (December 1978).

'Marital breakdown in the light of changing attitudes', *Midwife, Health Visitor and Community Nurse* (May 1979).

'Sex therapy', *Vogue* (April 1981).

'Marital stress in early years', *Health Visitor* (February 1982).

'Marriage counselling', *Psychiatry in Practice* (October 1982).

'Religion and the young, I and II', *The Sunday Press* (October 1985).

'An interview with Jack Dominian', *The Grail* (1986 (2)).

'Marriage as a continuing sacrament', *Teilhard Review* (Spring 1987).

'Human and divine love', *Teilhard Review* (Spring 1987).

'Marital breakdown and the Church', *Priests and People* (September 1987).

'Christianity and divorce', *Church Times* (April 1988).

'Sexuality: from law and biology to love and person', *The Grail* (1988 (4)).

'What is human development for priests?', *Priests and People* (December 1990).

'Sexuality and the family', *Studies in Christian Ethics, Sexual Ethics*, vol. 4 no. 2 (1991).

'Marriage: growth and decline', *The Furrow* (February 1992).

'The domestic Church', *Living Stones* (March 1992).

'Christian marriage', *The Catholic Herald* (August 1992).

Articles in *The Tablet*

'Challenge to Christian marriage' (20 September 1969).

'Marriage as a relationship' (27 September 1969).

'Marital breakdown' (4 October 1969).
'Modern marriage within the Church' (11 October 1969).
'The achievement of Alfred Adler' (7 February 1970).
'The permissive bishop' (14 March 1970).
'The Church and the sexual revolution' (24 October 1970).
'The nature of sexuality' (31 October 1970).
'Growing towards marriage' (7 November 1970).
'Sexuality in marriage' (14 November 1970).
'Sexual deviation' (21 November 1970).
'The single state' (28 November 1970).
'The power of positive love' (5 December 1970).
'Marriage, divorce and nullity' (24 April 1971).
'Conscience and marital breakdown: I' (19 June 1971).
'Conscience and marital breakdown: II' (26 June 1971).
'Conscience and marital breakdown: III' (3 July 1971).
'Authority and growth: I' (17 June 1972).
'Authority and growth: II' (24 June 1972).
'After the Longford Report' (11 November 1972).
'The end of sex' (18 November 1972).
'The end of sex' (25 November 1972).
'The end of sex' (2 December 1972).
'The single state: I' (10 August 1973).
'The single state: II' (17 August 1973).
'Cycles of affirmation' (20 October 1973).
'Cycles of affirmation' (27 October 1973).
'Cycles of affirmation' (3 November 1973).
'Cycles of affirmation' (10 November 1973).
'Nuns on television' (2 August 1975).
'Marital breakdown' (4 October 1975).
'Religion and conscience' (31 January 1976).
'Religion and conscience' (7 February 1976).
'Religion and conscience' (14 February 1976).
'Christians and sex: I' (20 November 1976).
'Christians and sex: II' (27 November 1976).
'Sex outside marriage' (4 December 1976).
'Sex outside marriage' (11 December 1976).
'The crisis of love' (1 January 1977).
'Authority and maturity: the roles of home and school' (13 May 1978).
'Authentic freedom' (24 June 1978).
'Authentic freedom' (1 July 1978).
'Responsible love' (10 February 1979).
'Marriage matters' (17 February 1979).
'The family today' (7 July 1979).
'Permanency in marriage' (21 July 1979).

'Faithfulness in marriage' (11 August 1979).

'Marriage and children' (18 August 1979).

'Marriage as sacrament' (29 September 1979).

'An open letter to the Synod' (30 August 1980).

'Love of self' (28 February 1981).

'Rejection of self' (7 March 1981).

'Love of neighbour' (14 March 1981).

'Loving our neighbour' (28 March 1981).

'Five minutes with the Pope' (20 February 1982).

'The meaning of suffering' (10 July 1982).

'Maintaining a relationship' (17 July 1982).

'Understanding ourselves' (24 July 1982).

'The Christian experience' (31 July 1982).

'The enemy of love' (19 March 1983).

'Through science to faith' (30 April 1983).

'The need for self-love' (7 May 1983).

'Loving our neighbour' (14 May 1983).

'Christian marriage' (4 February 1983).

'The use of sex' (11 February 1983).

'The scourge of divorce' (18 February 1983).

'Domestic sacrament' (25 February 1983).

'*Humanae Vitae* revisited' (27 October 1984).

'*Humanae Vitae* revisited II' (3 November 1984).

'*Humanae Vitae* revisited III' (10 November 1984).

'*Humanae Vitae* revisited IV' (17 November 1984).

'Religion and the young: the third Church' (31 August 1985).

'The God we need' (7 September 1985).

'The sacrament of marriage' (14 September 1985).

'The significance of sex' (21 September 1985).

'The way ahead' (28 September 1985).

'Chastity' (8 March 1986).

'AIDS and morality' (10 January 1987).

'The domestic church' (4 April 1987).

'A revolution in context: sexual morality today' (9 January 1988).

'The scourge of divorce' (16 January 1988).

'The challenge of AIDS' (23 January 1988).

'The theology of sex' (30 January 1988).

'A sickness in society' (2 July 1988).

'Failures in love: the modern face of sin' (10 March 1990).

'Priesthood and marriage' (17 November 1990).

'A Kinsey Report on the priesthood' (19 January 1991).

'Cohabitation and marriage' (June 1992).

One Plus One Publications

B. Thornes and J. Collard, *Who Divorces?* (London: Routledge and Kegan Paul, 1979).

J. Brannen and J. Collard, *Marriages in Trouble* (London: Tavistock Publications, 1982).

P. Mansfield and J. Collard, *The Beginning of the Rest of Your Life* (London: Macmillan, 1988).

J. Dominian, P. Mansfield, D. Dormor, F. Mcallister, *Marriage and Partnership Breakdown: What You Can Do To Help* (London: One Plus One, 1990).

Marital Breakdown and the Health of the Nation (London: One Plus One, 1991).

D. Dormor, *The Relationship Revolution* (London: One Plus One, 1992).

Selected Unpublished Dominian Talks

'Values in marriage: change and continuity'.

'Christian marriage' (delivered at a private conference of the Brenninkmeyer Family, Zurich, 7–9 July 1989), and question and answer session typescript.

Various talks on 'Christian marriage'.

'Marriage, divorce and the family' — talk given during The Marriage Research Centre's Conference on 'Marriage, Divorce and the Family' (1984).

'A review of 50 marital problems'.

'Marital breakdown in the light of changing sexual attitudes'.

'Marriage research centre'.

'Institute for the family'.

'Questions on family life'.

Spode House talks:
   'Capacity to love — love of self' (February 1981).
   'Maintaining a relationship' (June 1982).
   'The meaning of suffering' (June 1982).
   'Guilt' (June 1986).
   'Guilt and relationship' (June 1986).

'Marital breakdown and the future of marriage'.

'The centrality of love in the New Testament'.

'The contribution of psychology in the renewal of faith'.

'A psychological contribution to international trust'.

'What to put up with'.

'The history of AIDS'.

'Marital breakdown and society'.

'The stress of marital breakdown'.

'Help-seeking for marital difficulties'.

'Doctor as prophet'.

'Divorce in England and Wales'.
'Pilot survey into marriages celebrated in a Catholic church between the
     years 1960–1967'.
'Marriage and society'.
'The body and sexuality'.
'Continuity and change of values in marriage'.
'The health consequences of divorce'.
'Sexuality in the year 2000'.
'The significance of marital breakdown'.
'Communication in marriage'.
'Personal love and sin'.
'What is psychological healing?'.
'Clinical illustrations of counselling'.
'Patterns of marital breakdown'.
'Response to divorce'.
'The meaning of sexual intercourse in marriage'.
'Encountering myself: guilt and forgiveness'.
'The genetics of manic-depressive illness'.
'Being ourselves'.
'Only those who see the invisible can do the impossible'.
'Evangelization and the family'.
'Communication in marriage'.
'The changing nature of marriage'.
'Sexuality and the family'.
'The consequences of marital breakdown'.
'Human sexuality'.
'Life together'.
'Sexual behaviour in the early years of marriage'.
'Marriage and women'.
'The first Joseph Butler Memorial Lecture'.
'The emotional impact of children on parents'.
'Married love'.
'Problems in the early years of marriage'.
'Jesus' confrontation with evil — psychological aspects'.
'Trends in sexual behaviour — an evaluation'.
'Personality disorders'.
'Marriage counselling — English experience'.
'Trust and Russia'.
'Marital stress and affective disorder'.